All the designs in this coloring book has been created symmetrically around a center point. The relation of the constituents to a common center of stillness helps the mind to center itself and allows an observer's consciousness to easily entrain with the encryption of the mandalic depictions.

Interacting with the designs through coloring induces a calming and meditative effect due to various factors including, but not limited to, symmetry around a center and repetitiousness.

"One of the earliest scientists to have studied the therapeutic benefits of coloring pages for adults was Carl Jung. He studied coloring of Mandalas as early as the first half of the 20th century. He often used Mandalas (which have concentric circles and geometrical patterns in them) for his patients and found that it helped them become calmer and witness lesser stress." Writes Jacob Olesen on his website color-meanings.com in a description of "10 Therapeutic Benefits of Coloring Books For Adults".

Other scientifically researched benefits of coloring pages for adults include: increased mindfulness, activation of both parts of the cerebral hemisphere, being transported back to the stress free days of childhood, reduction in the chatter of a restless mind, reduction of anxiety (and consequently thoughts of death or dying, excessive worry, nausea, headaches, chills, fever, insomnia, etc.), re-discovery, becoming un-stuck from a rut, therapeutic effect on many diseases, inner child re-connection, being transported to a time and place faraway, and... it sparks creativity!

"One of the most important benefits of coloring books for adults is that they help ignite creativity which adults continue to experience in several other facets of their lives. Adults who color regularly find that they become great at picking colors for their clothes, their interiors etc. Coloring books and pages also help people become more creative in their jobs, analytical thinking activities and several other aspects of work and play." (Jacob Olesen). So, grab your colors and experience all these benefits first hand!

No rules, but to prevent bleed through we do recommend using a piece of paper behind the page you choose to dive into, and try to relax the back of your tongue, relax it some more, just really relax it... this helps your brainwaves to slow down and shift into alpha state.

FEEL GOOD COLORING BOOK

First published in the United States of America in 2016 by
Infinite808 Media
Charleston, SC

ISBN: 9781530623631

This book can be ordered from the Amazon websites or by contacting
the publisher directly at infinite808MEDIA@Gmail.com.

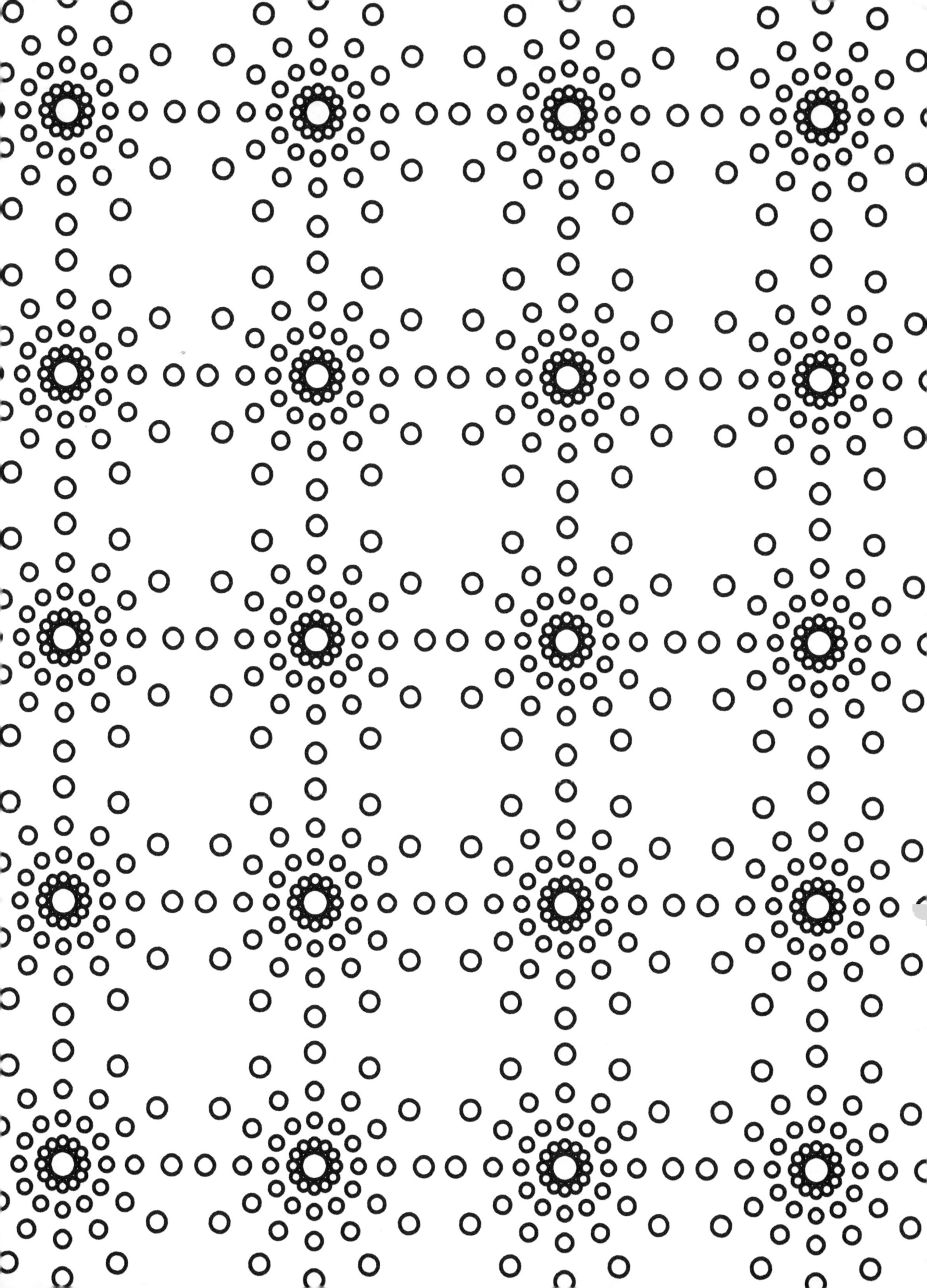

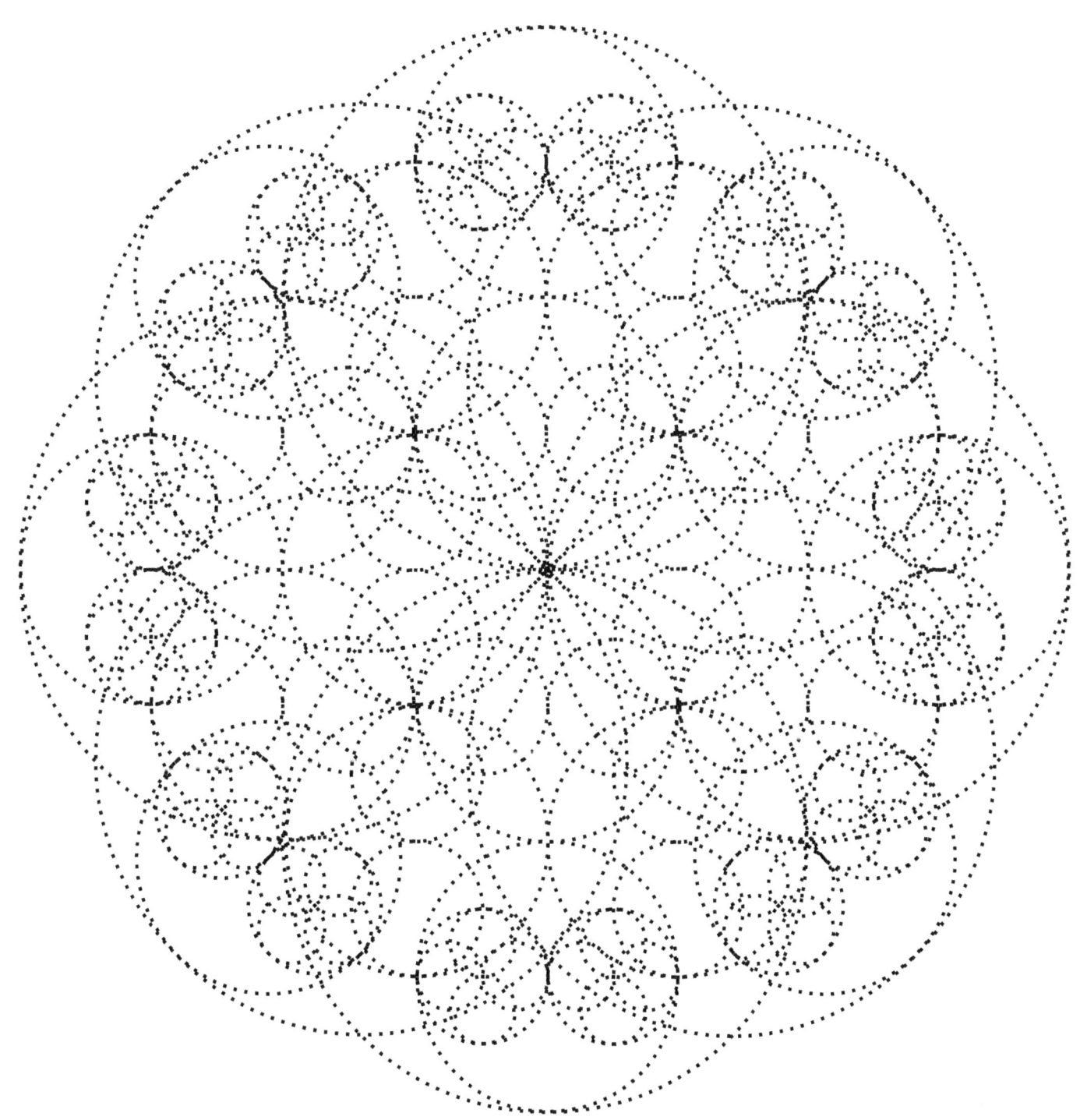

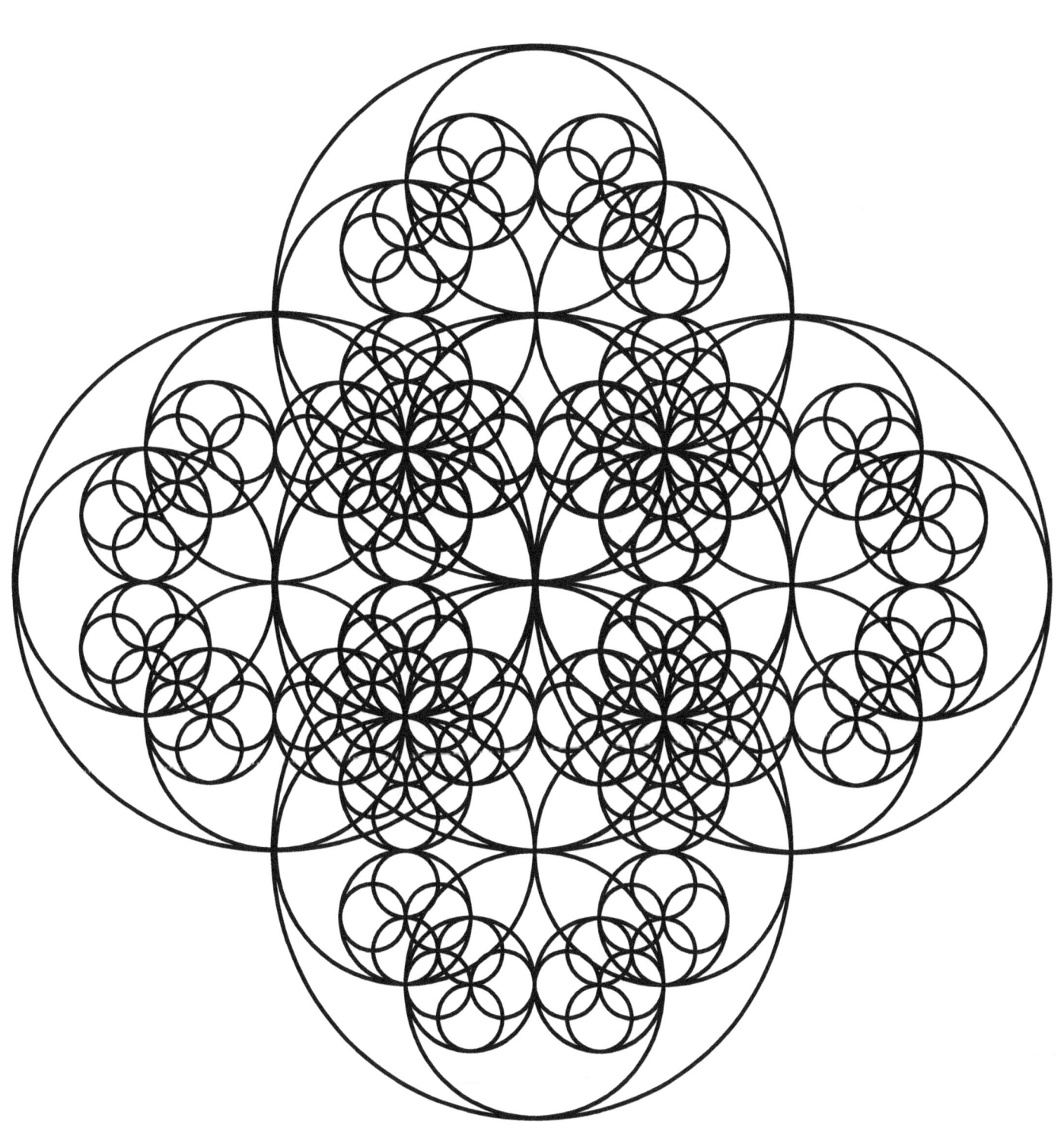

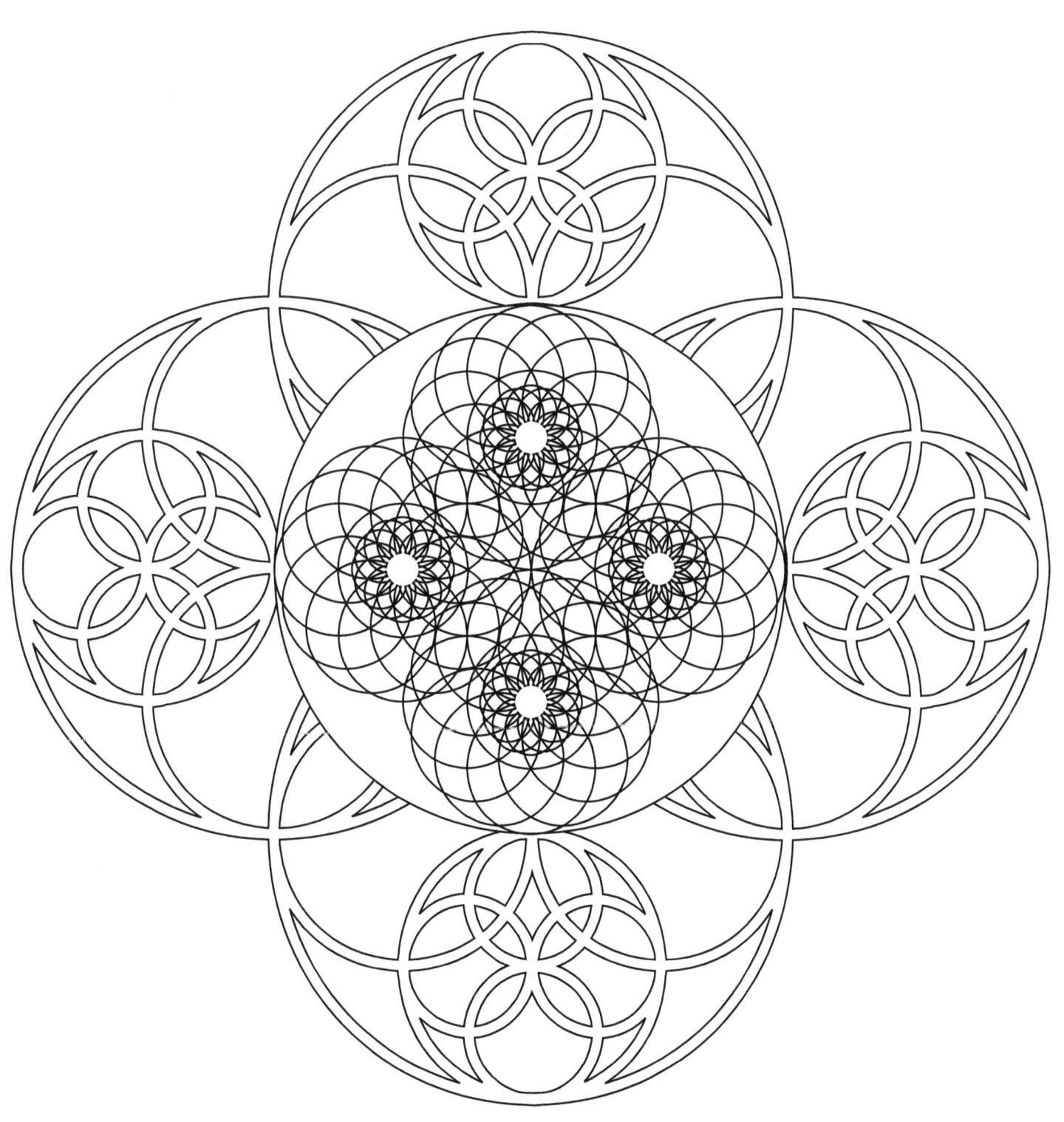

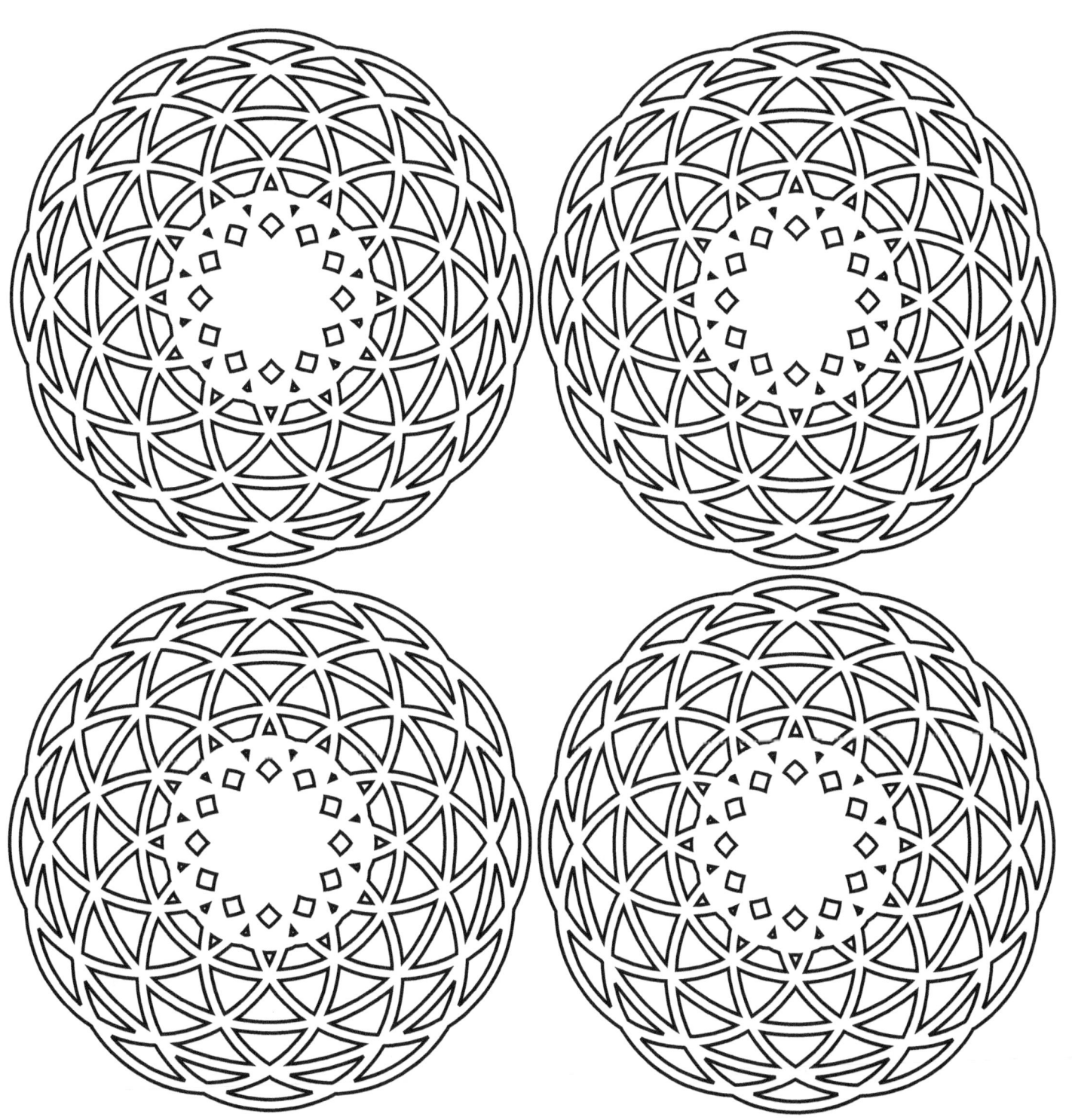

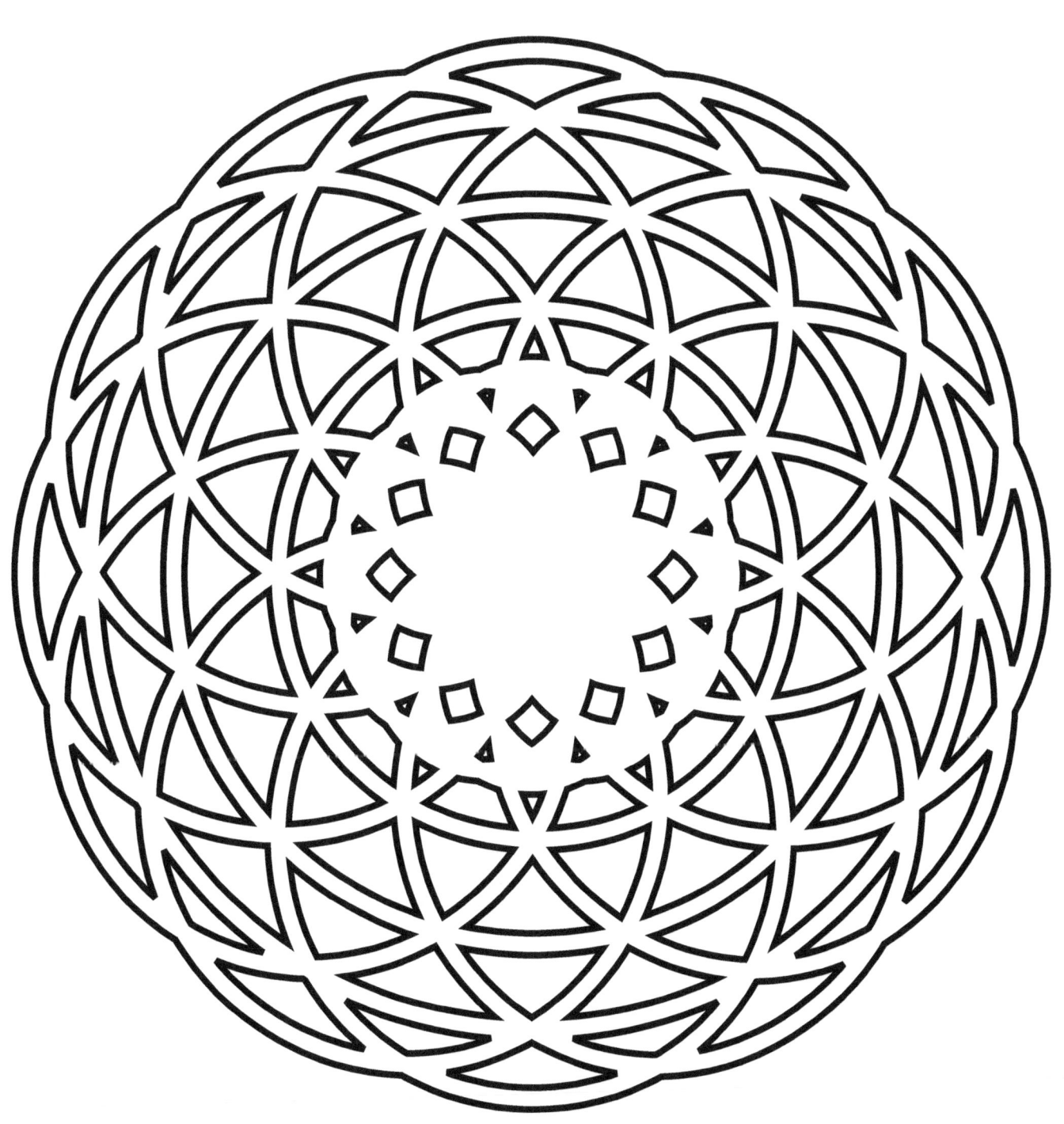

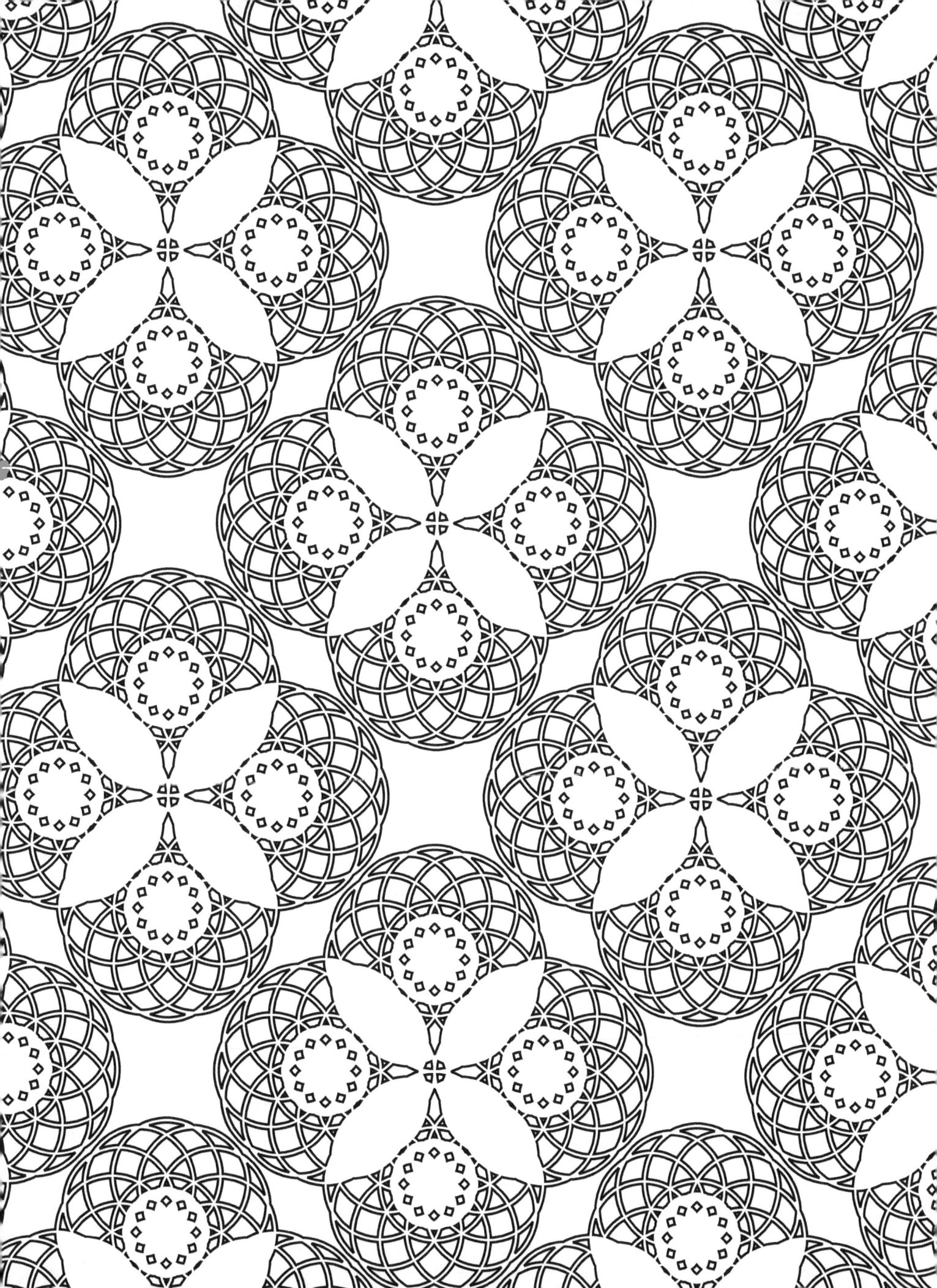

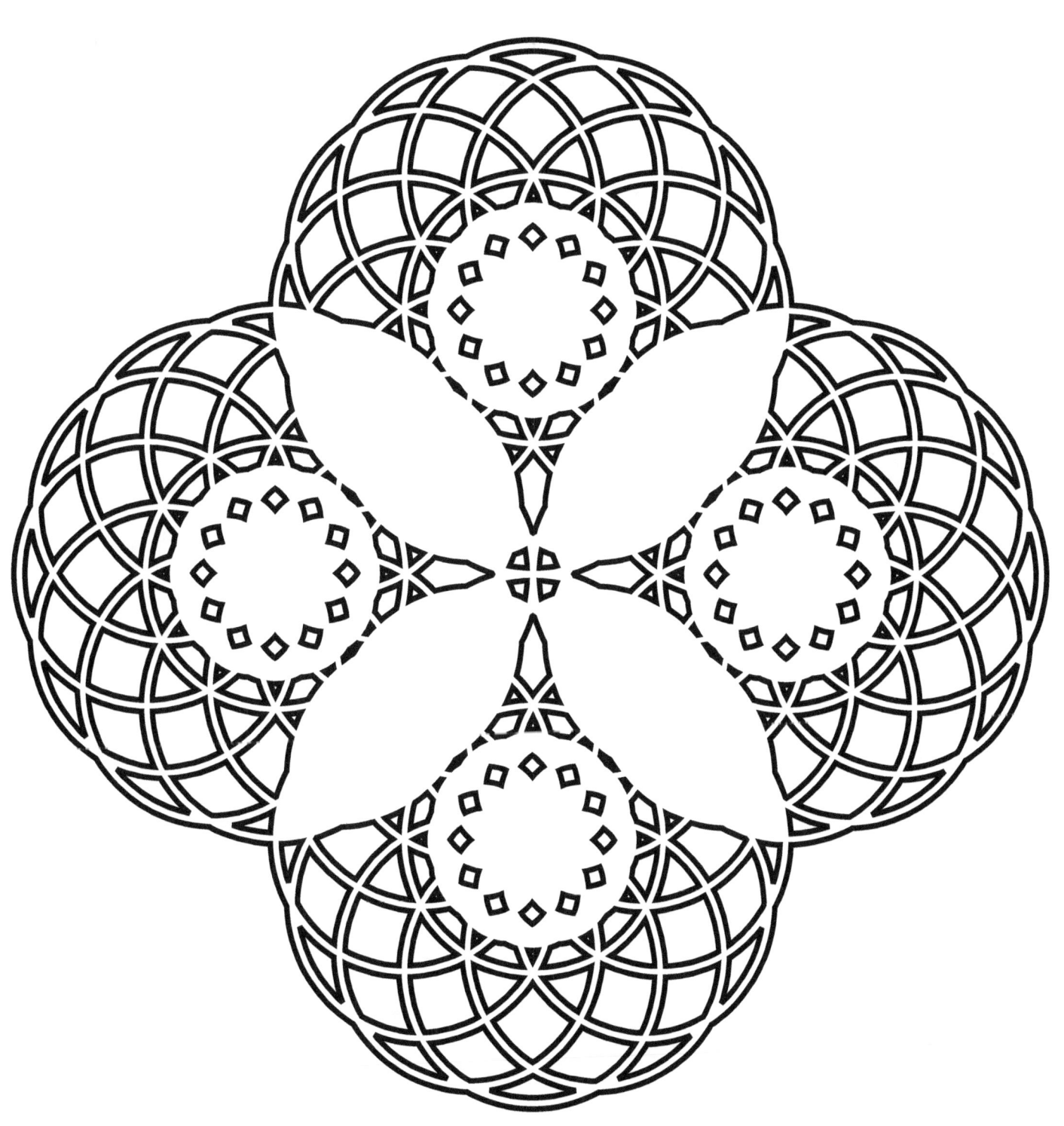

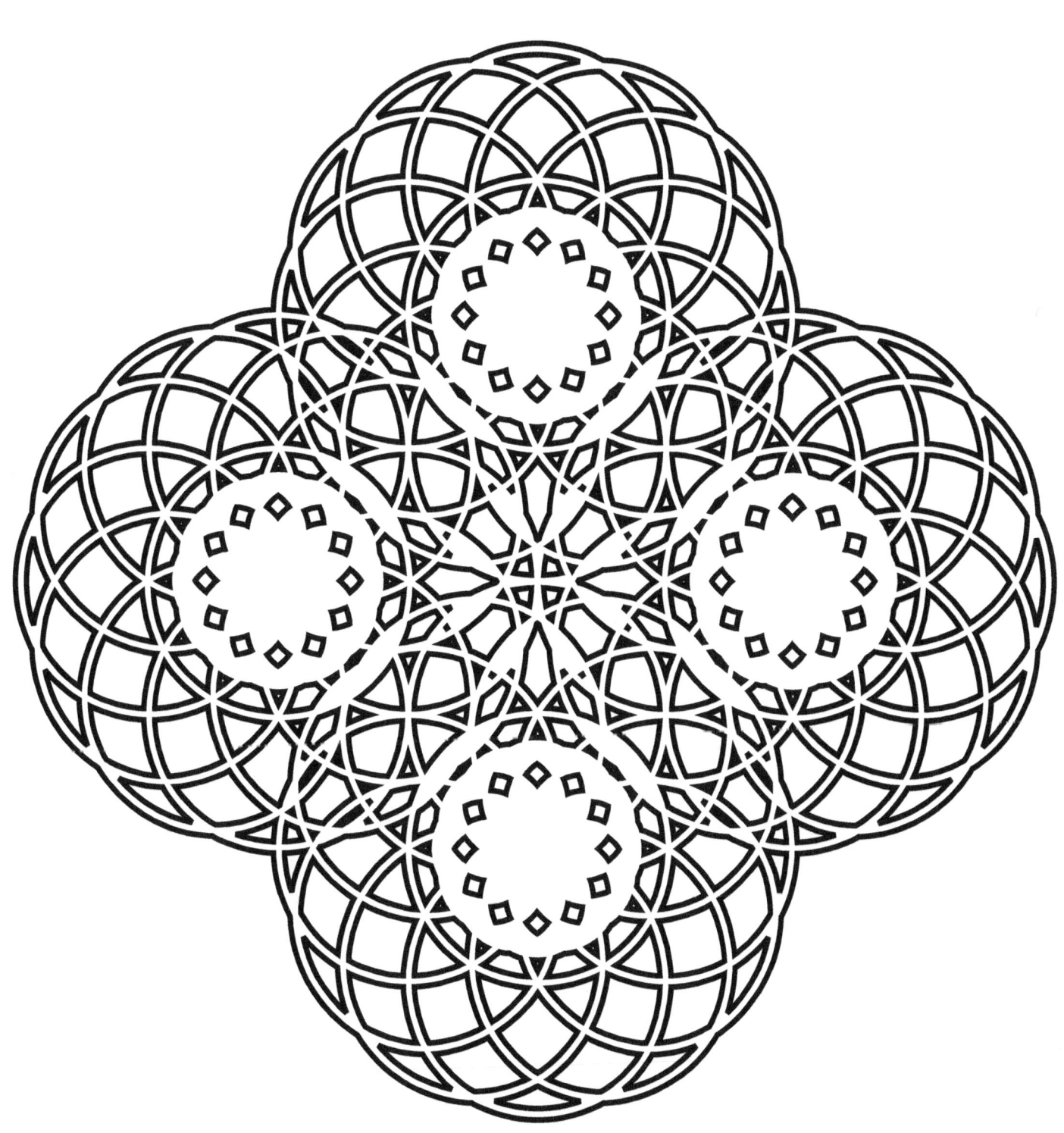

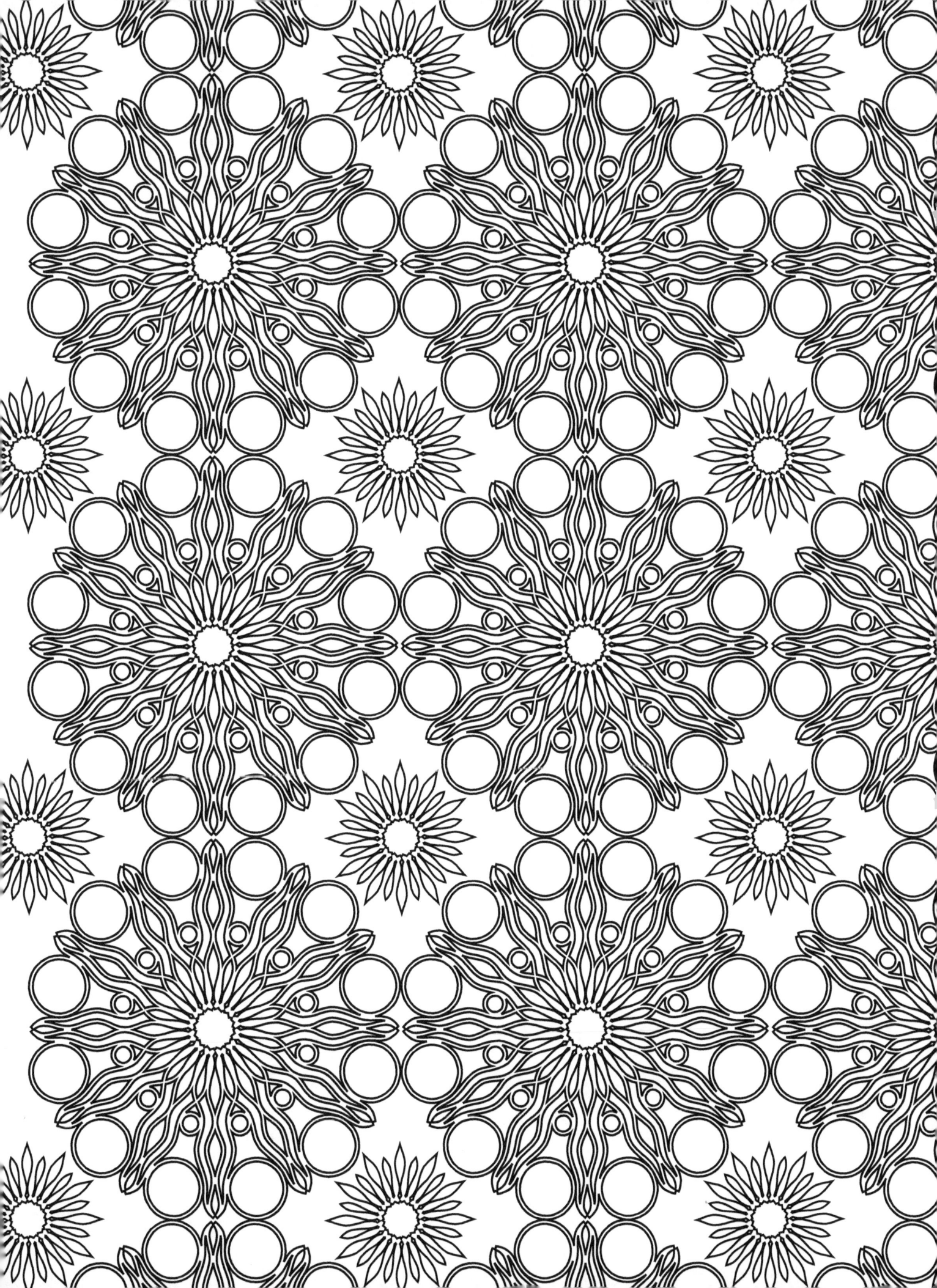

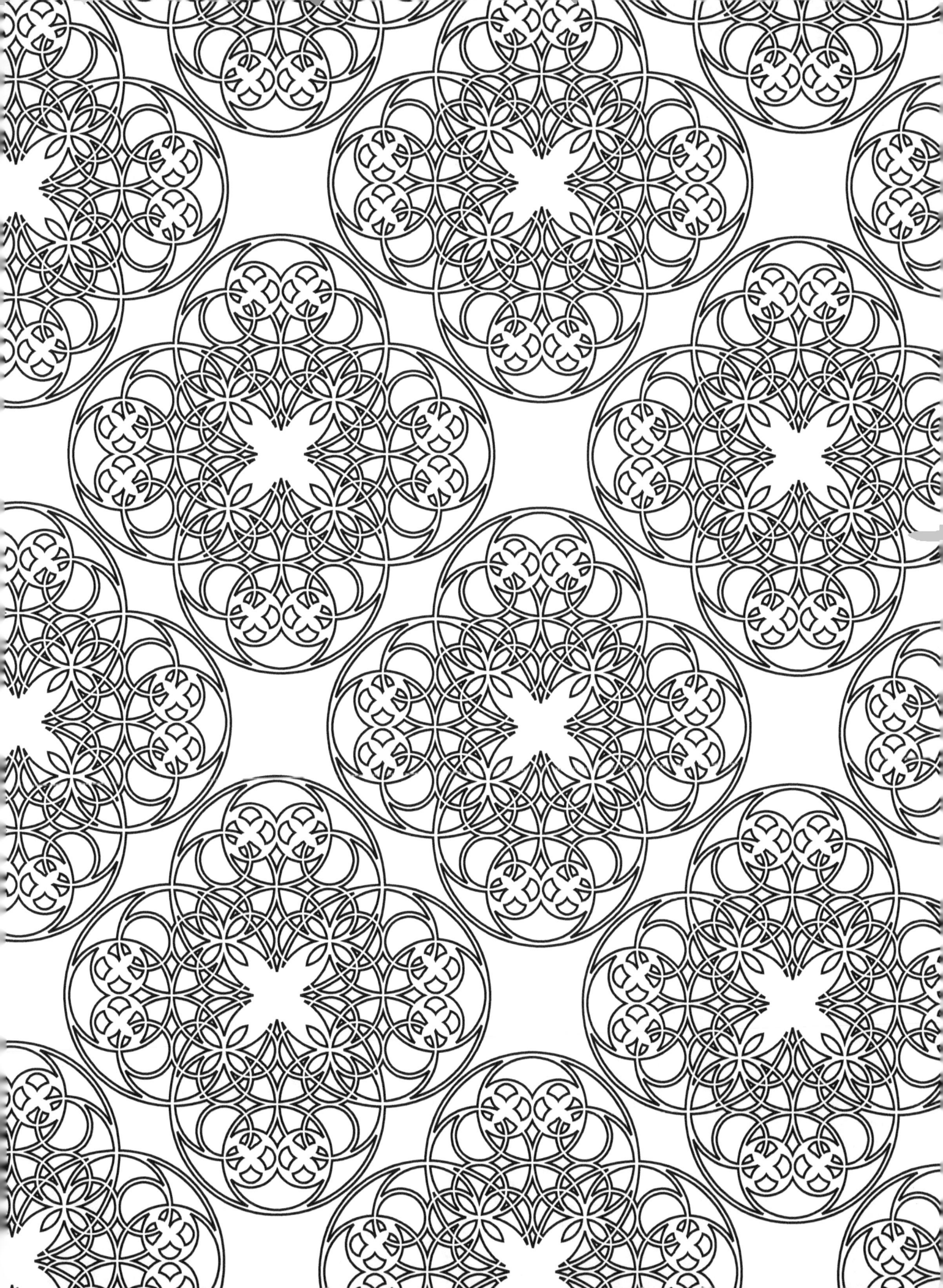

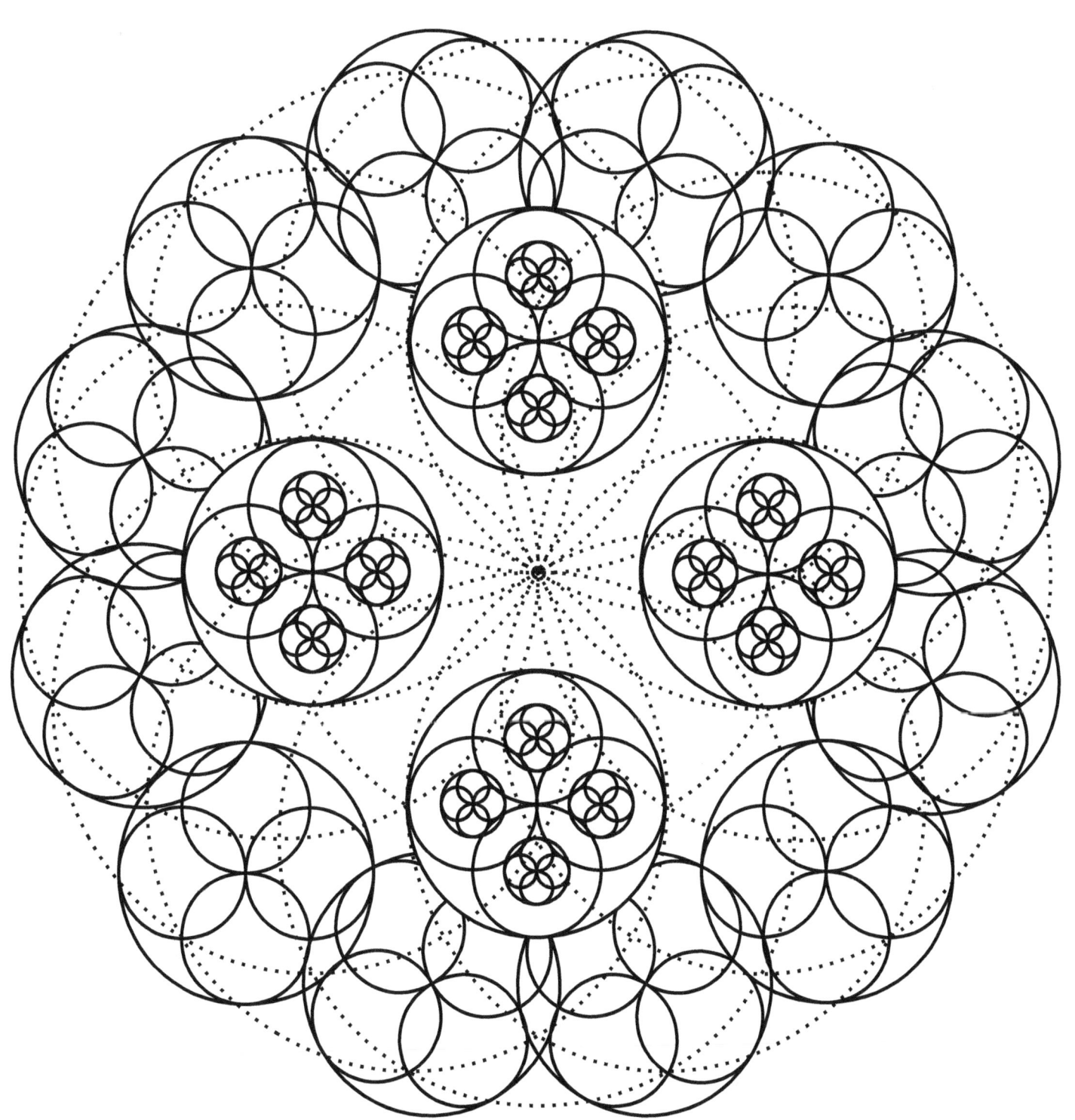

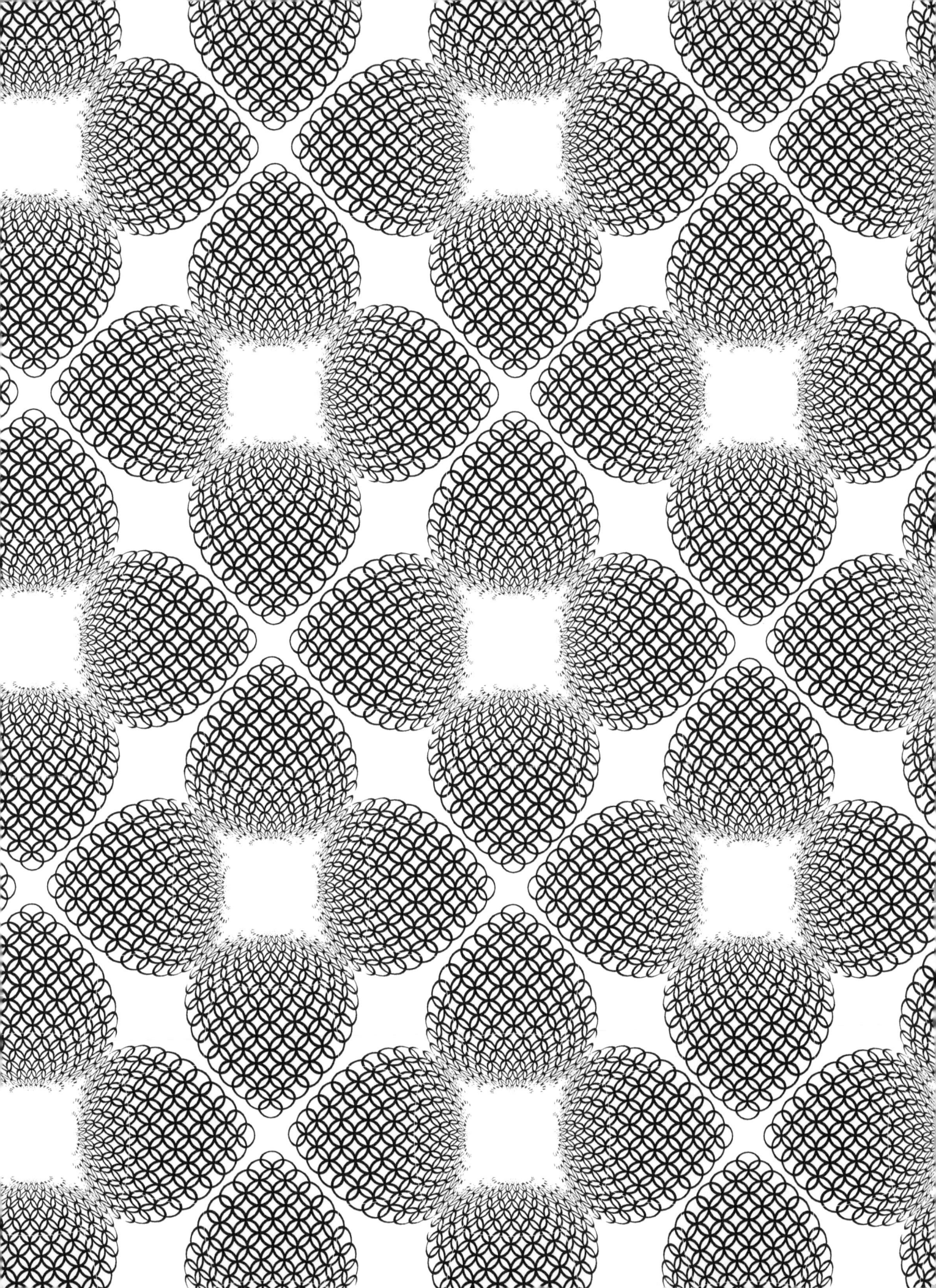

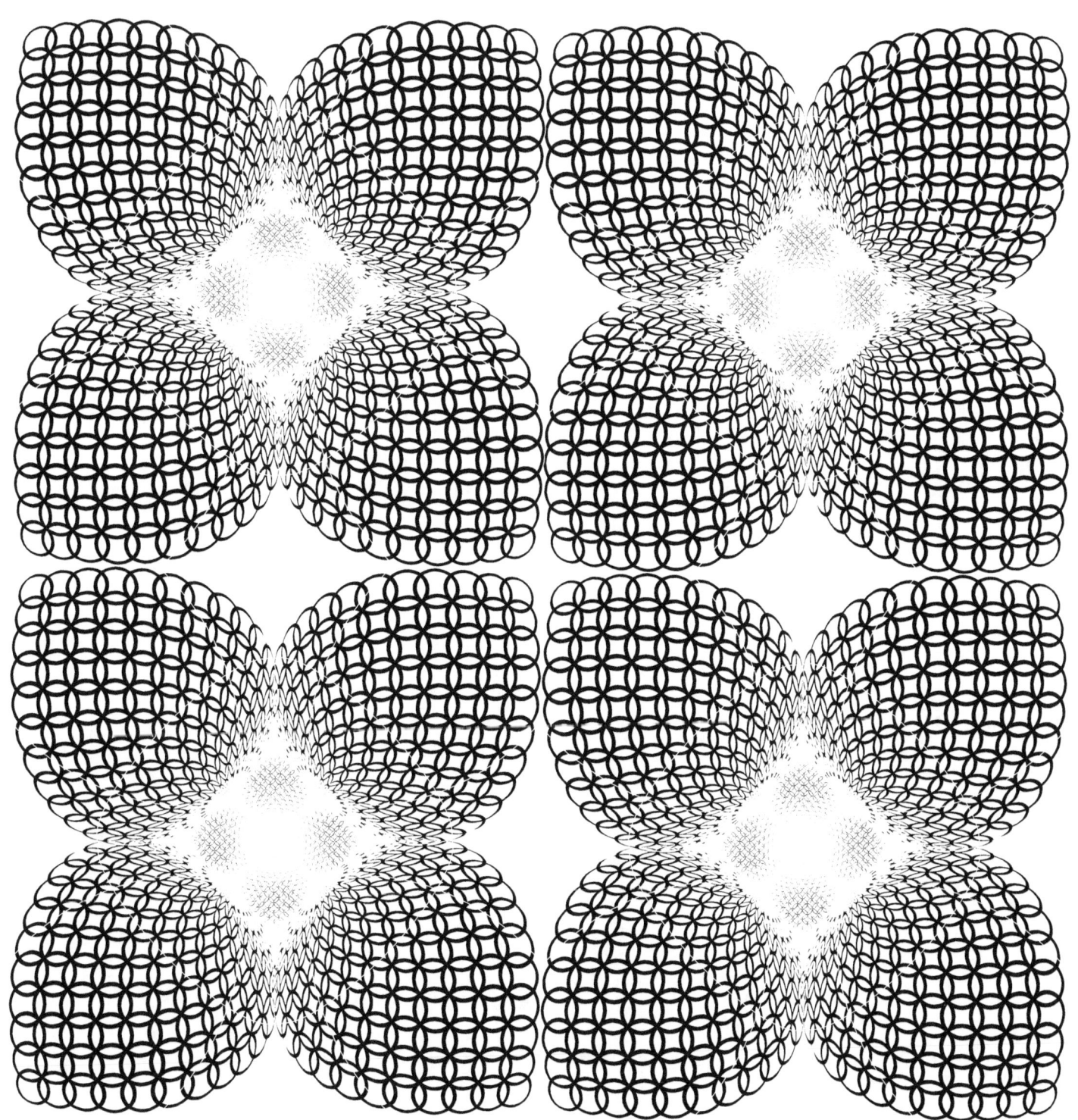

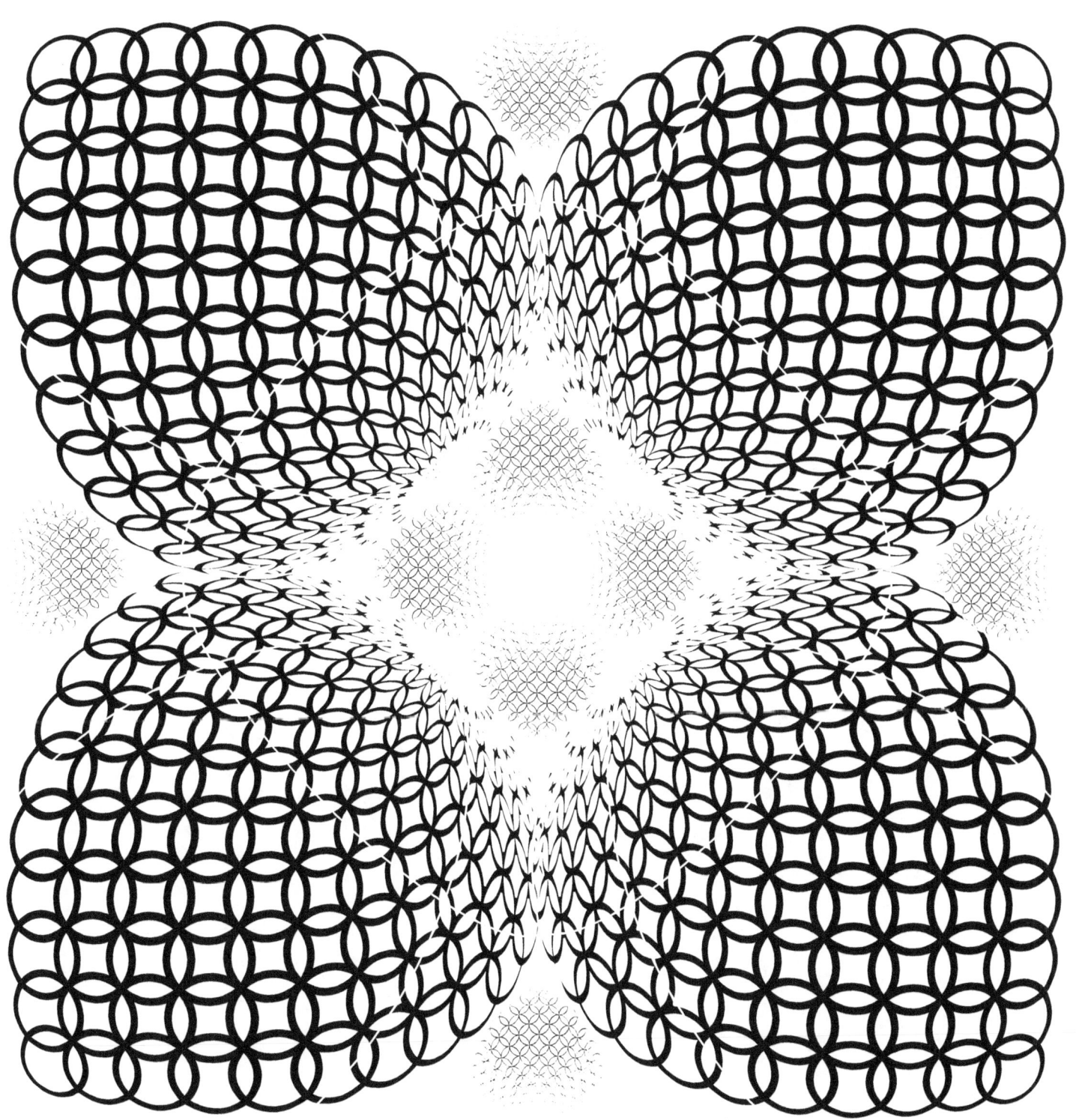

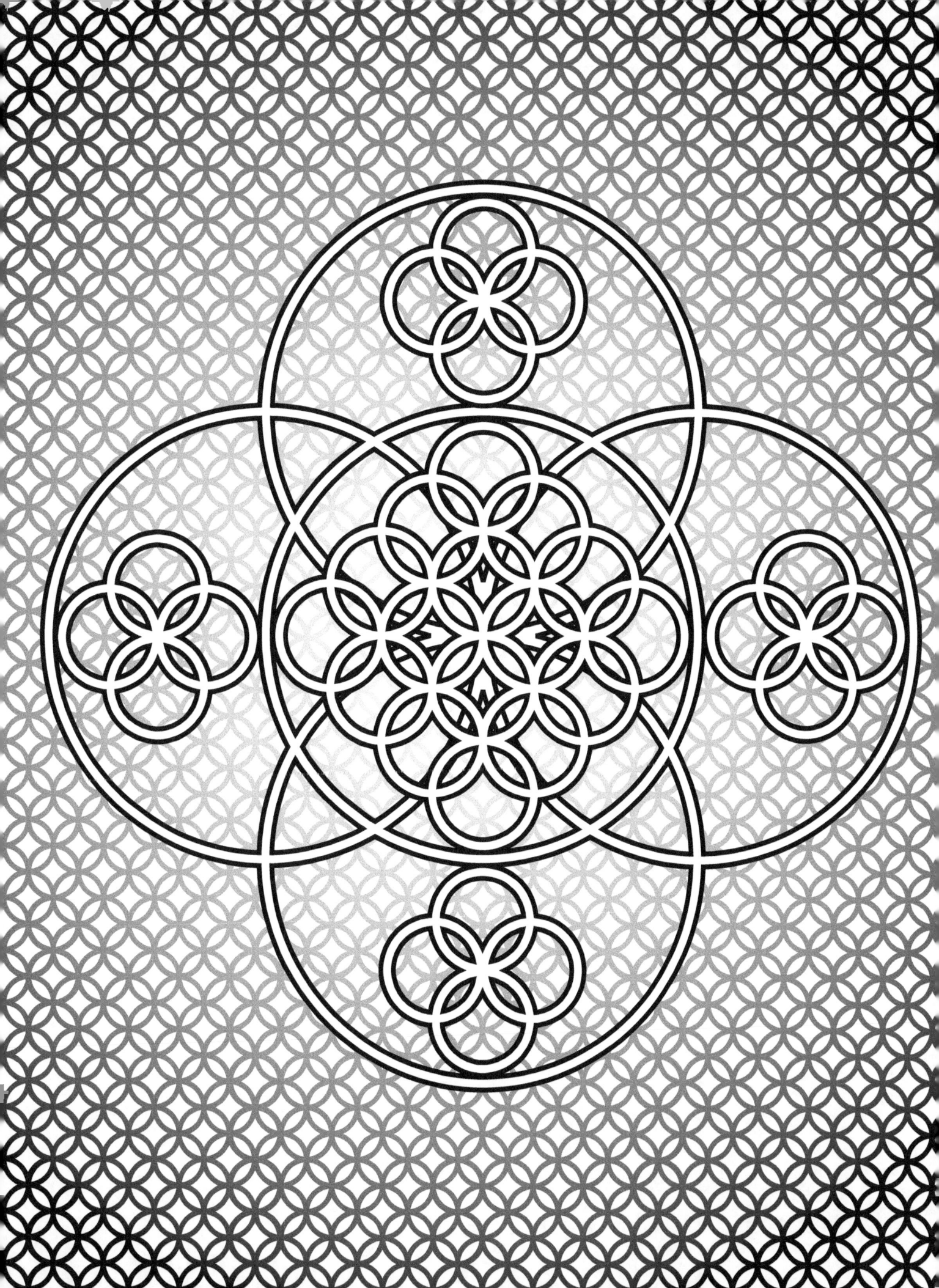

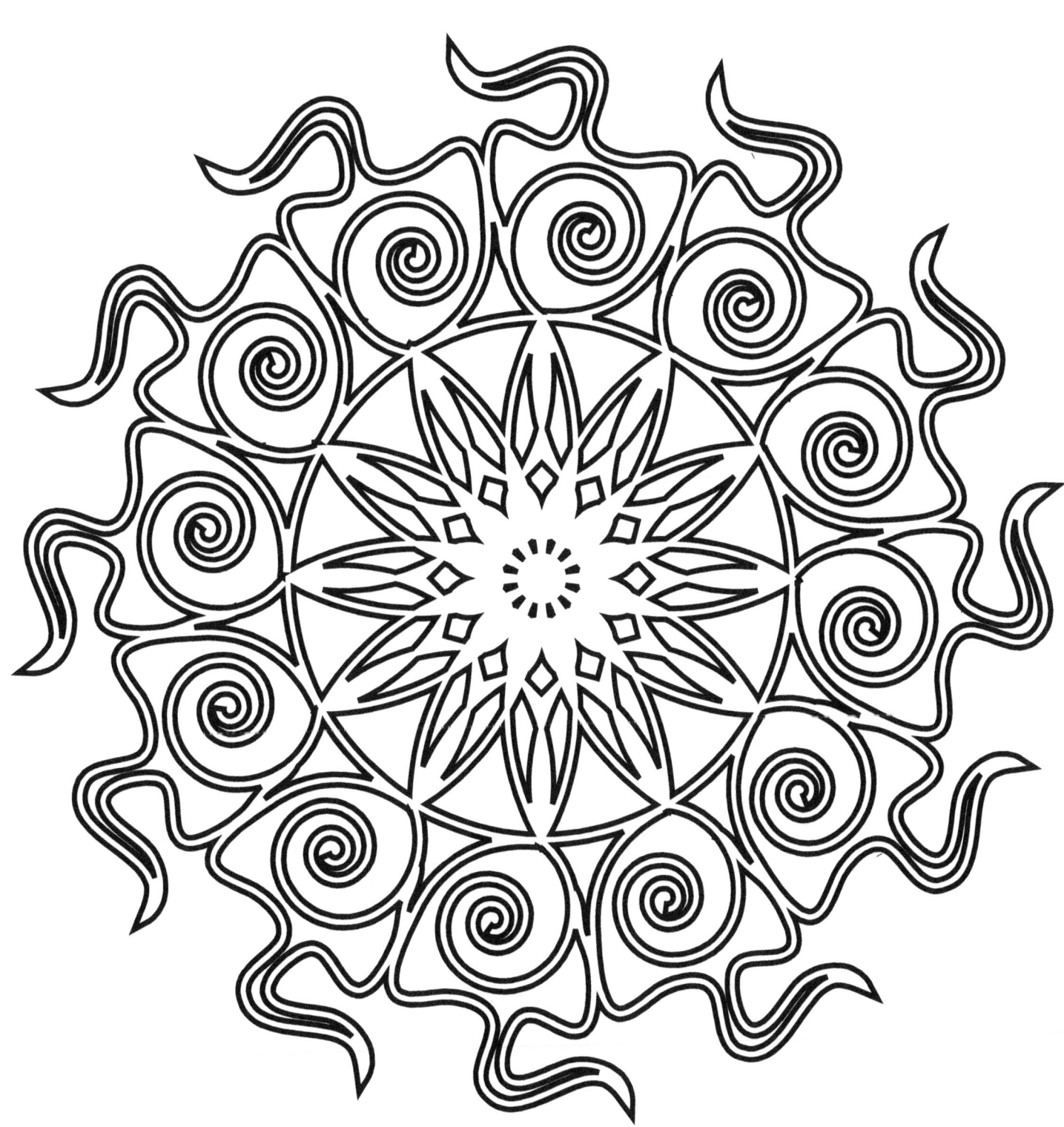

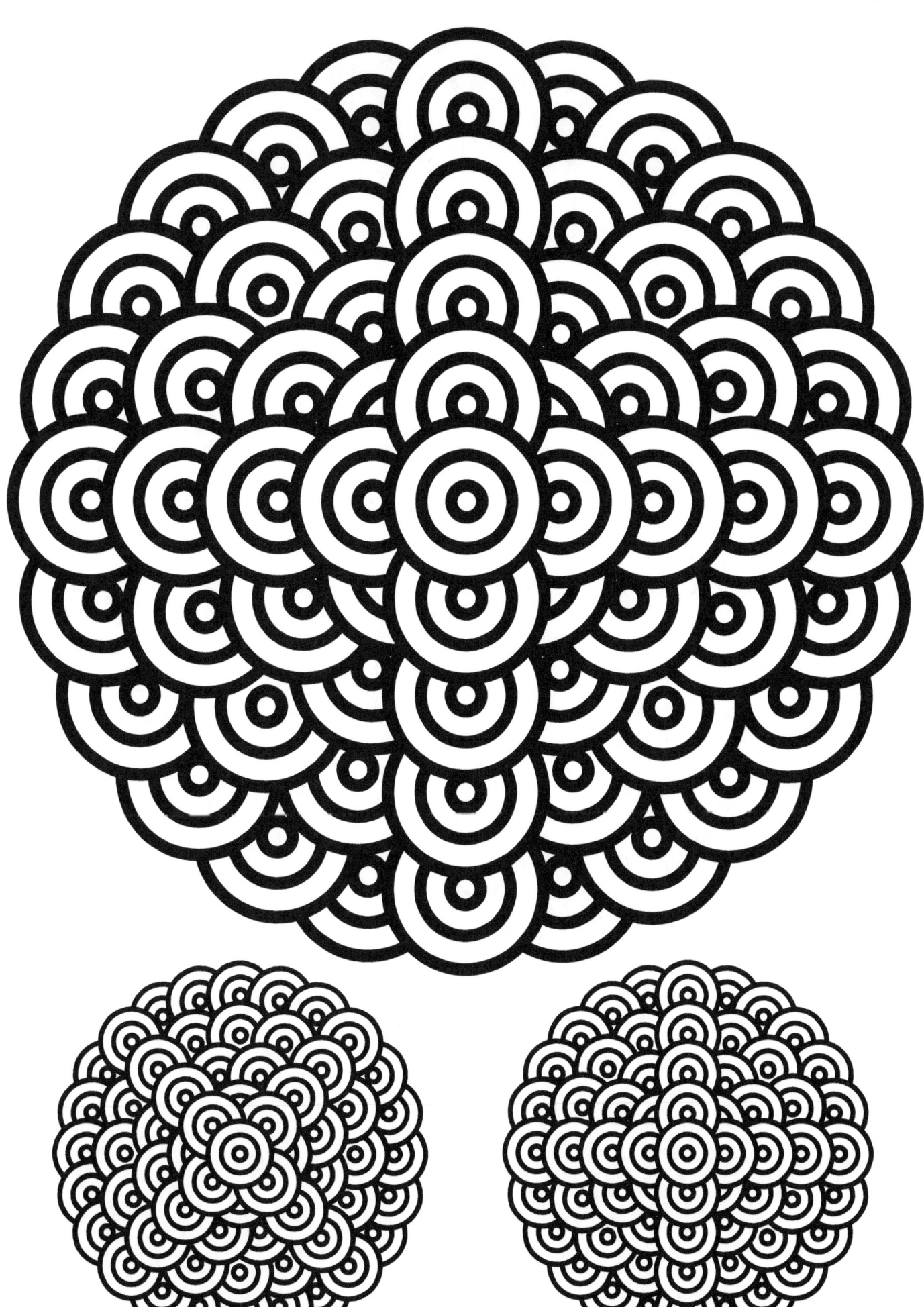

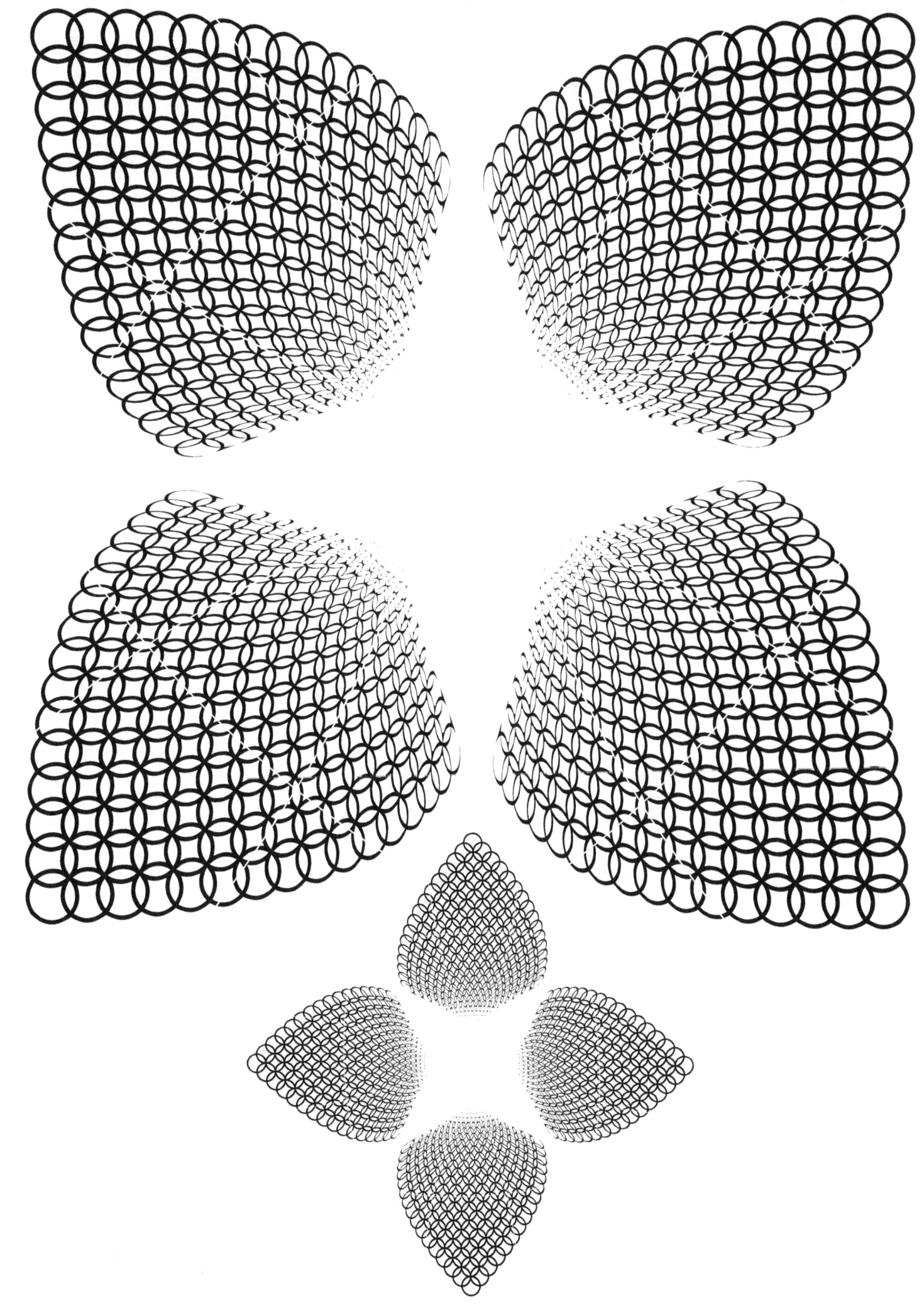

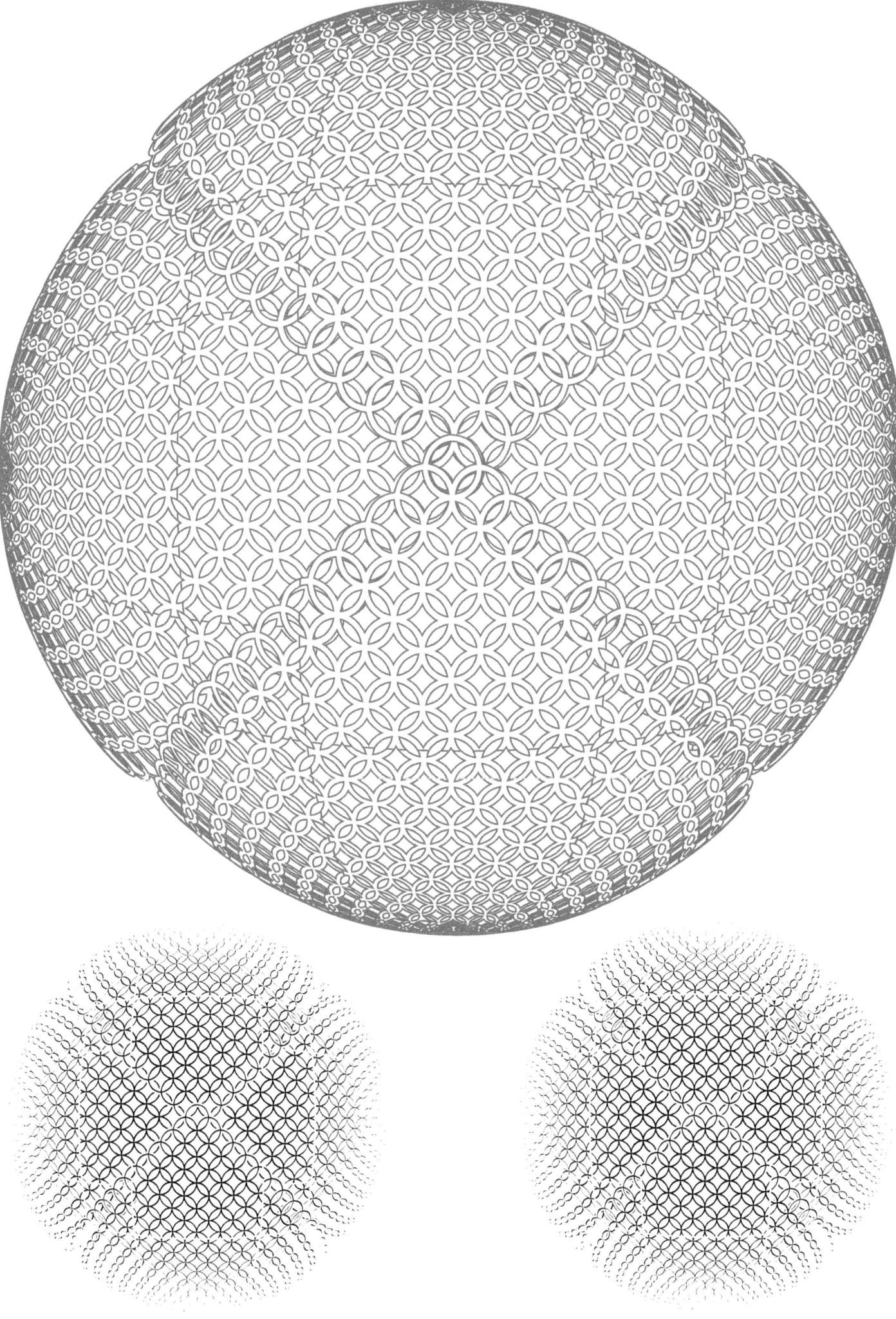

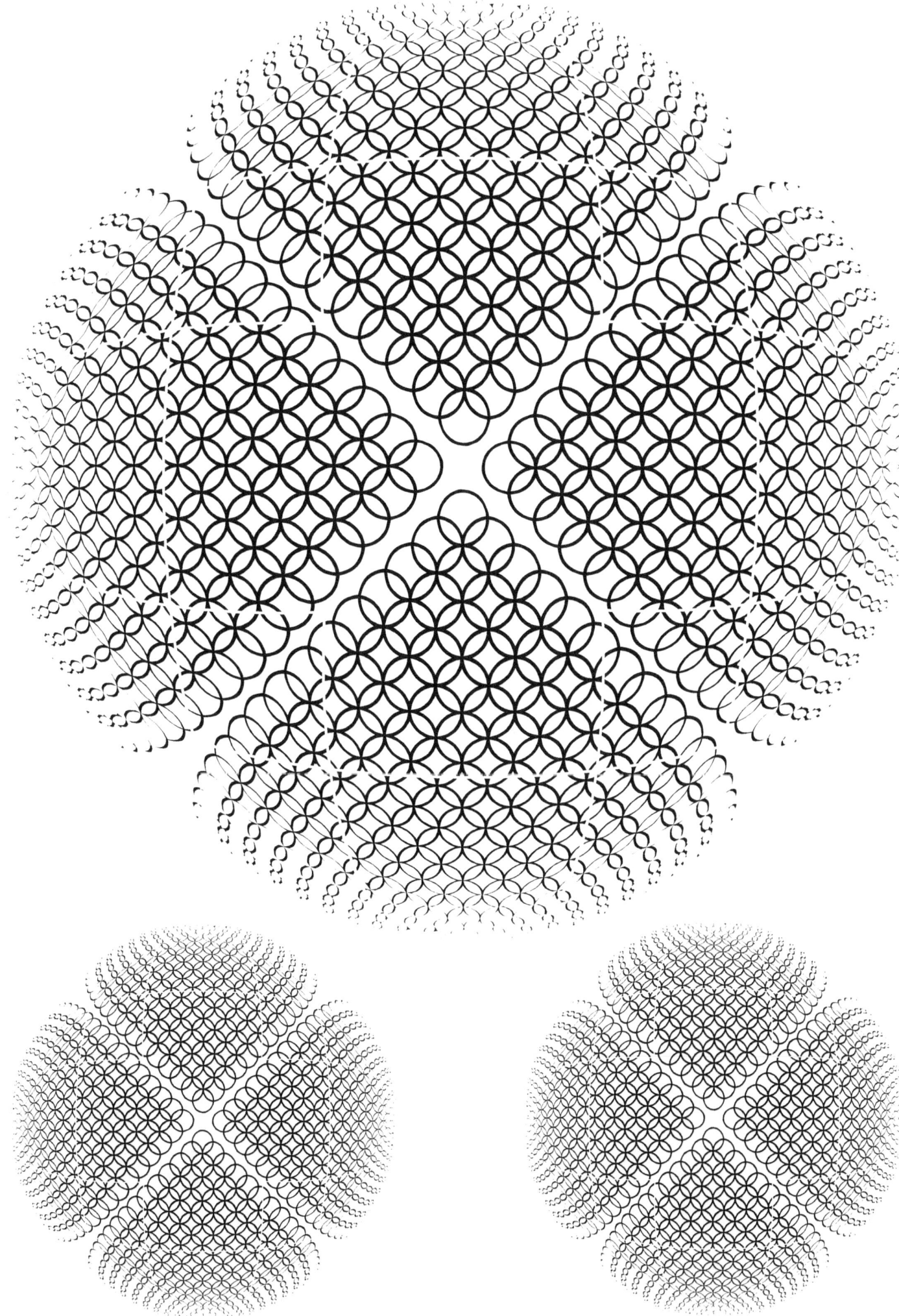

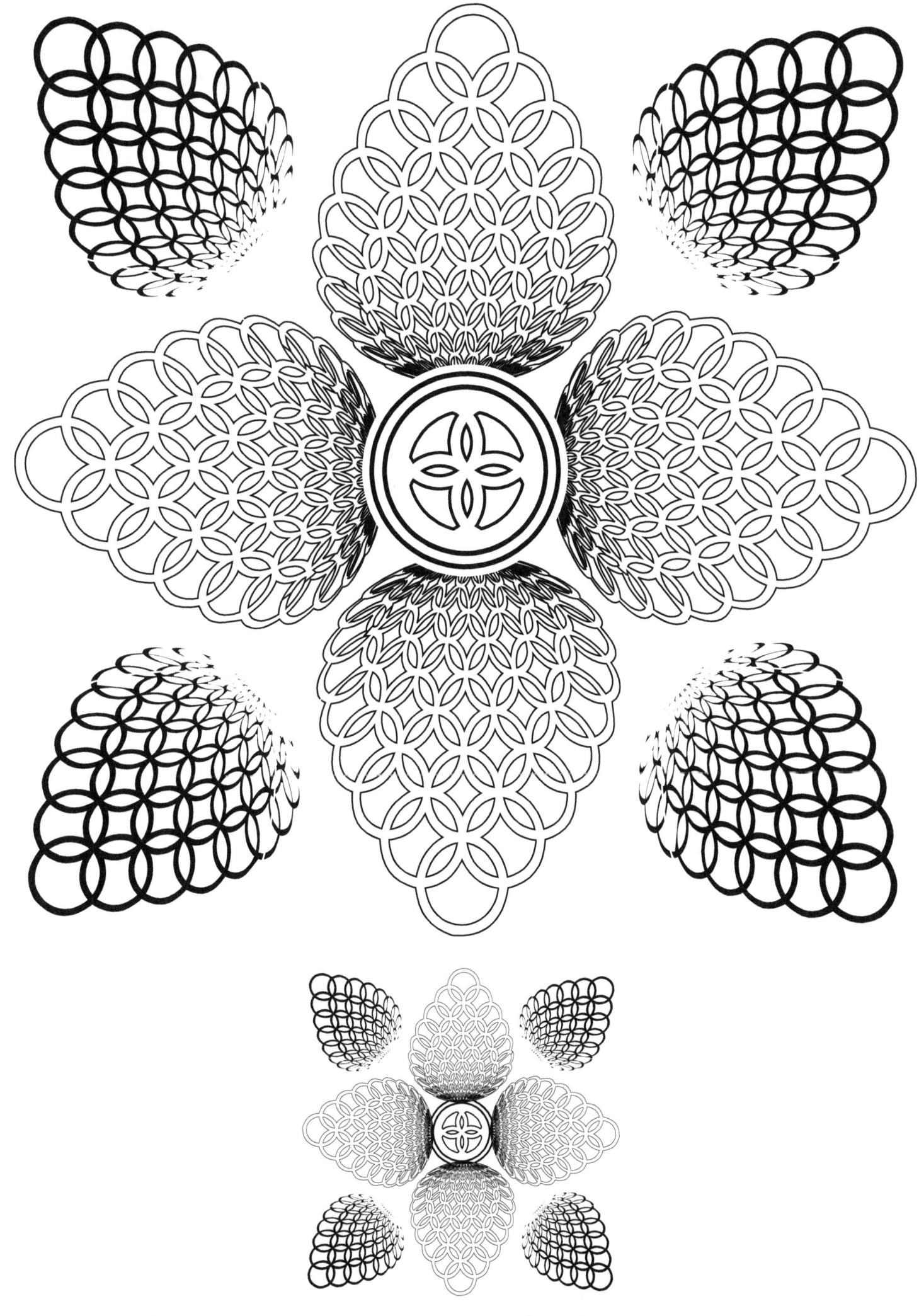

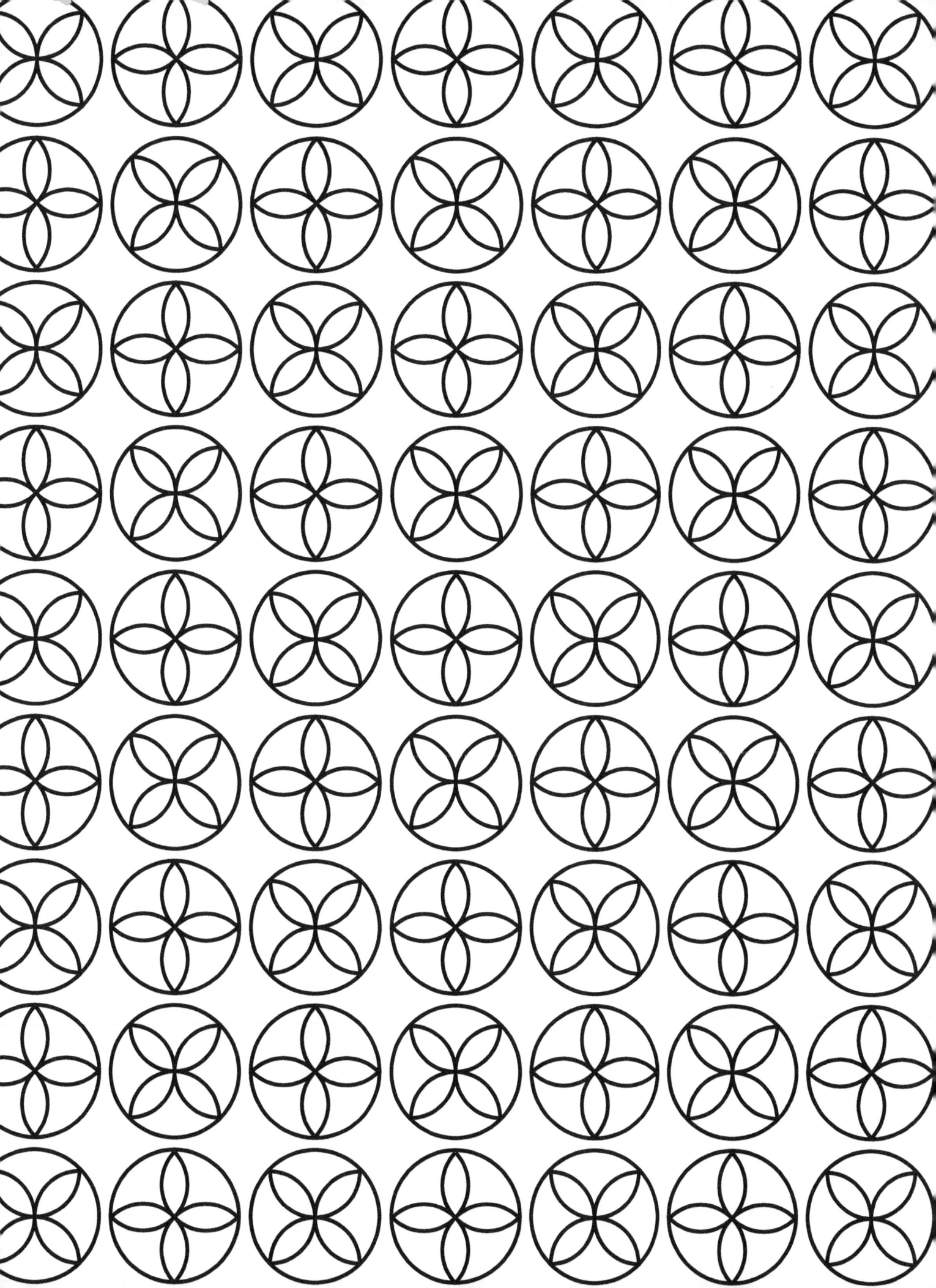

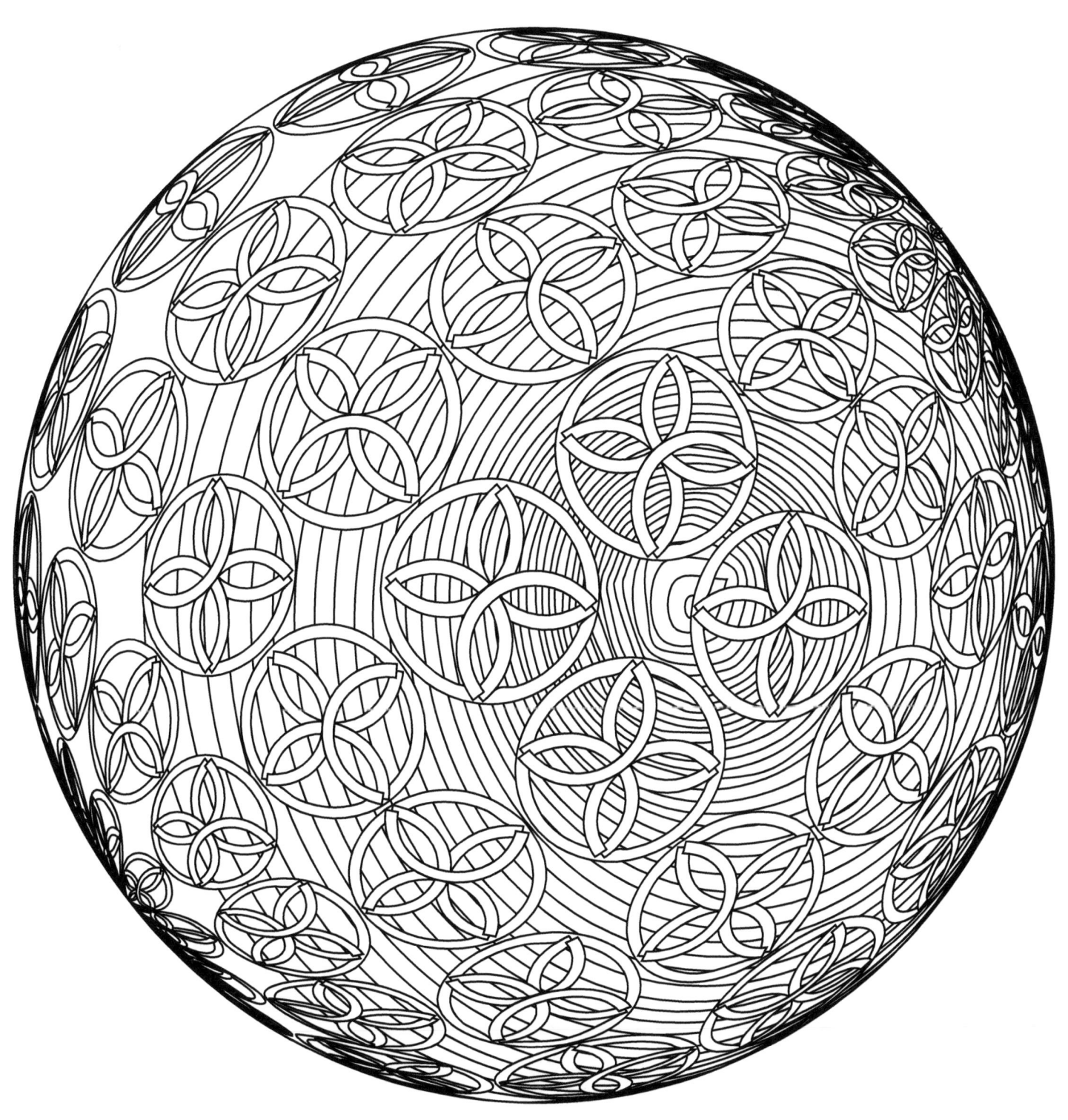

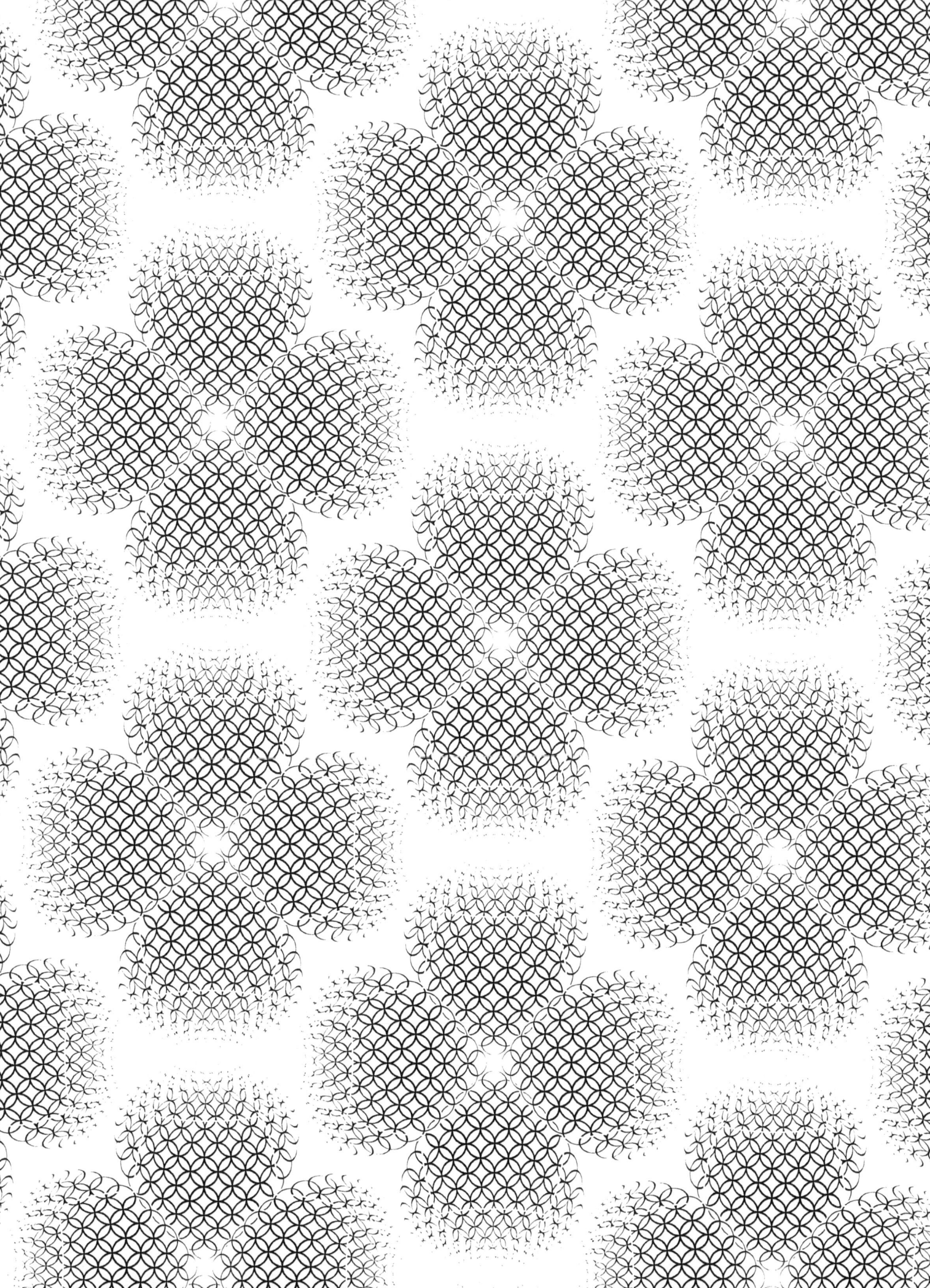

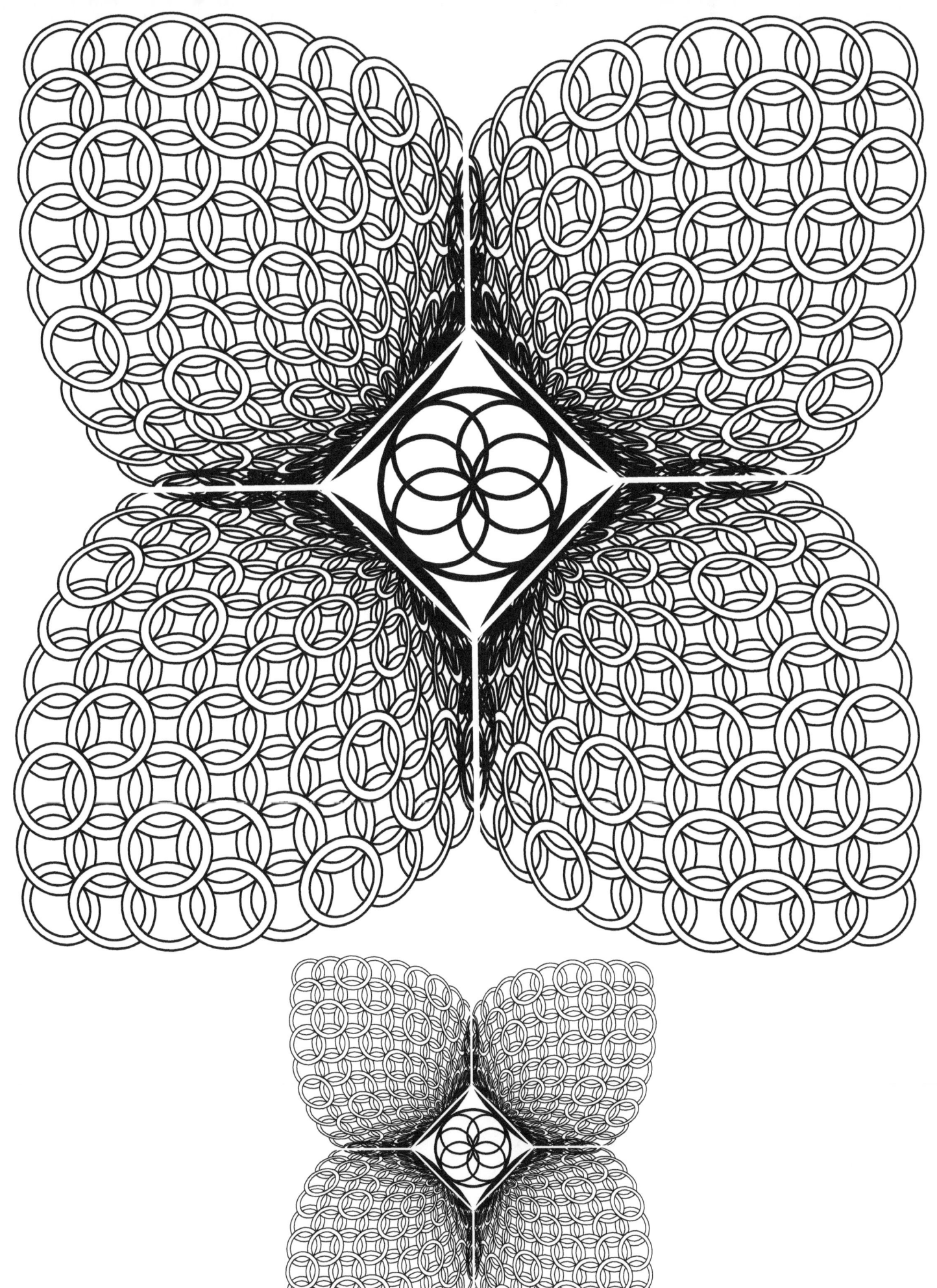

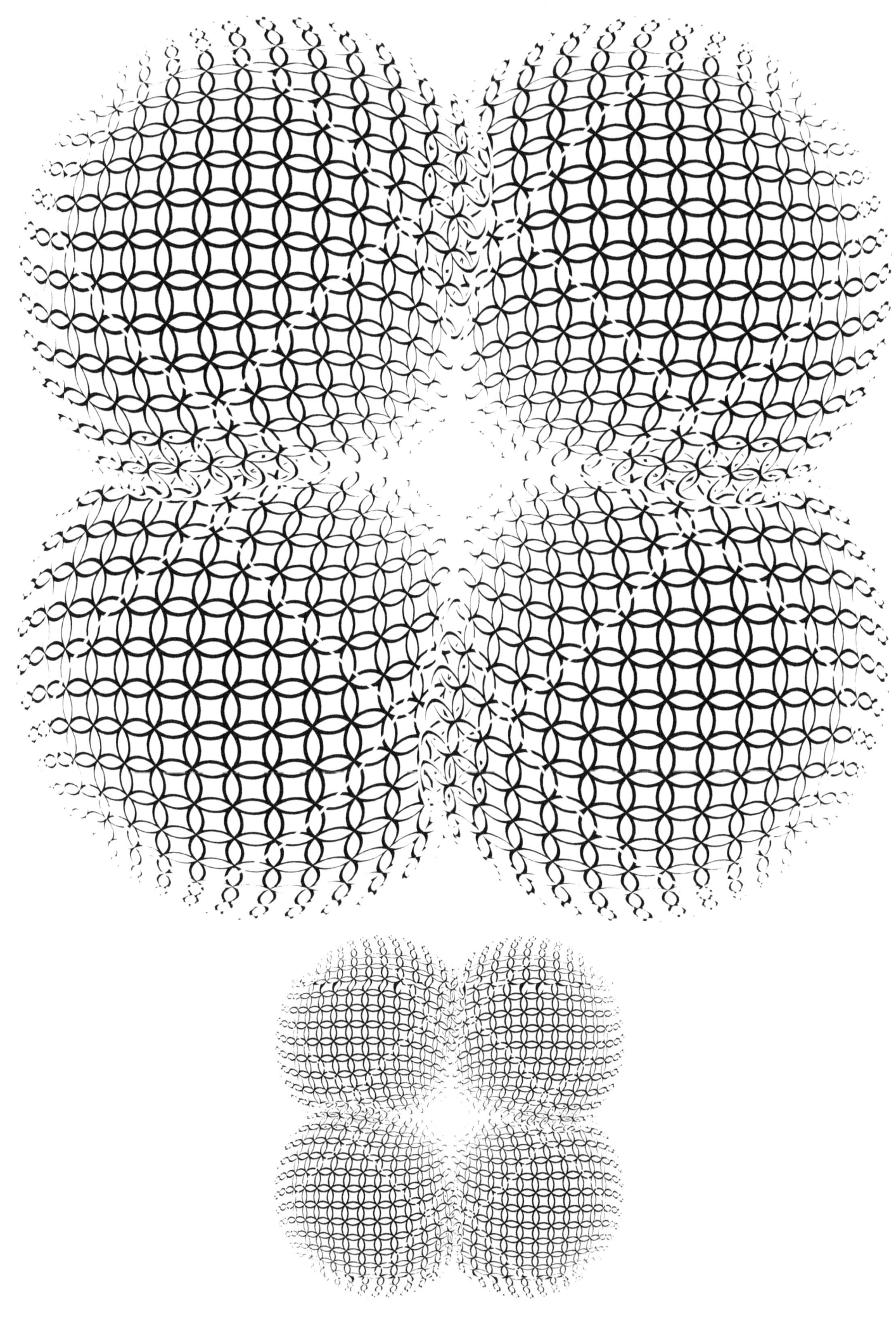

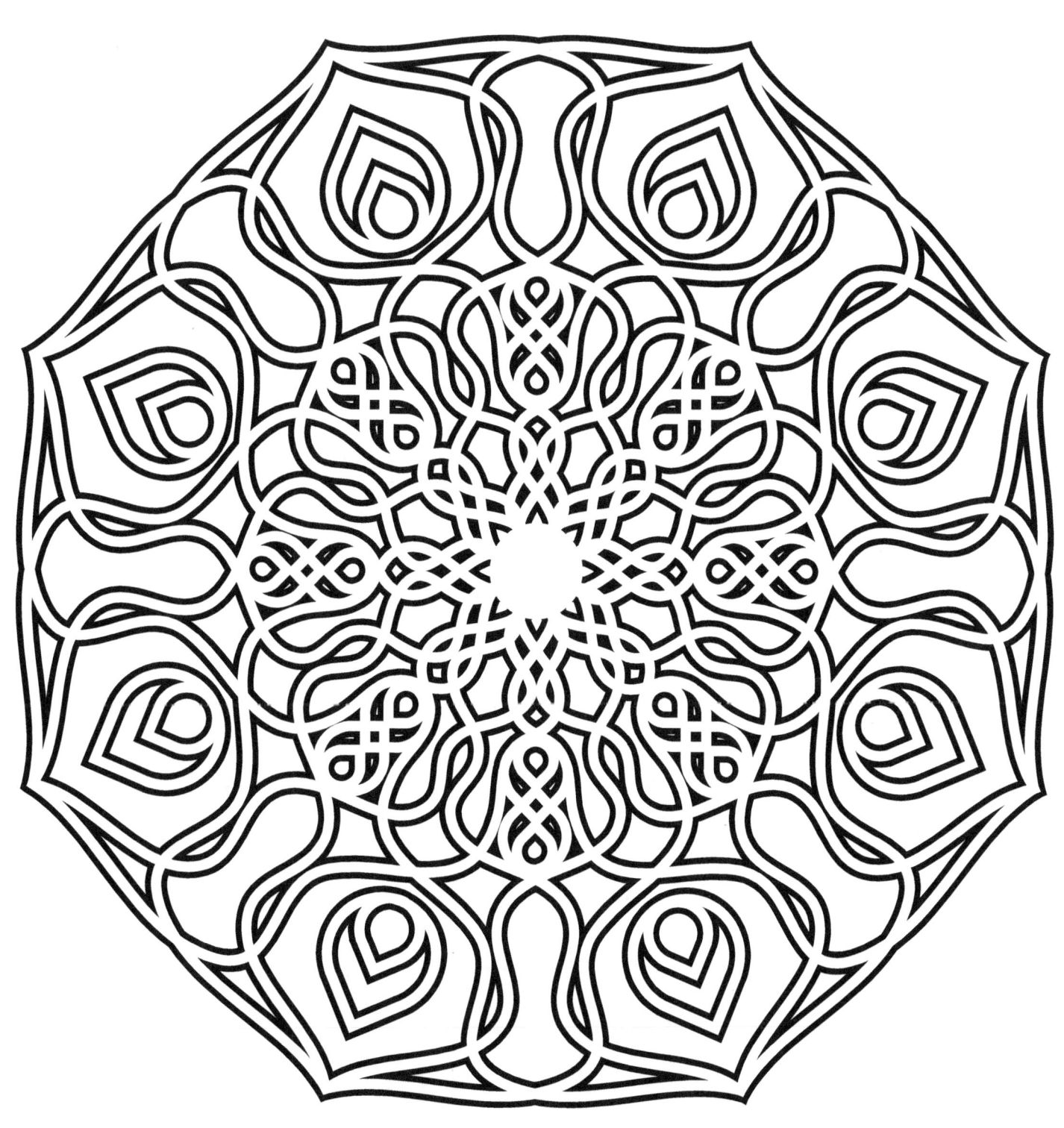

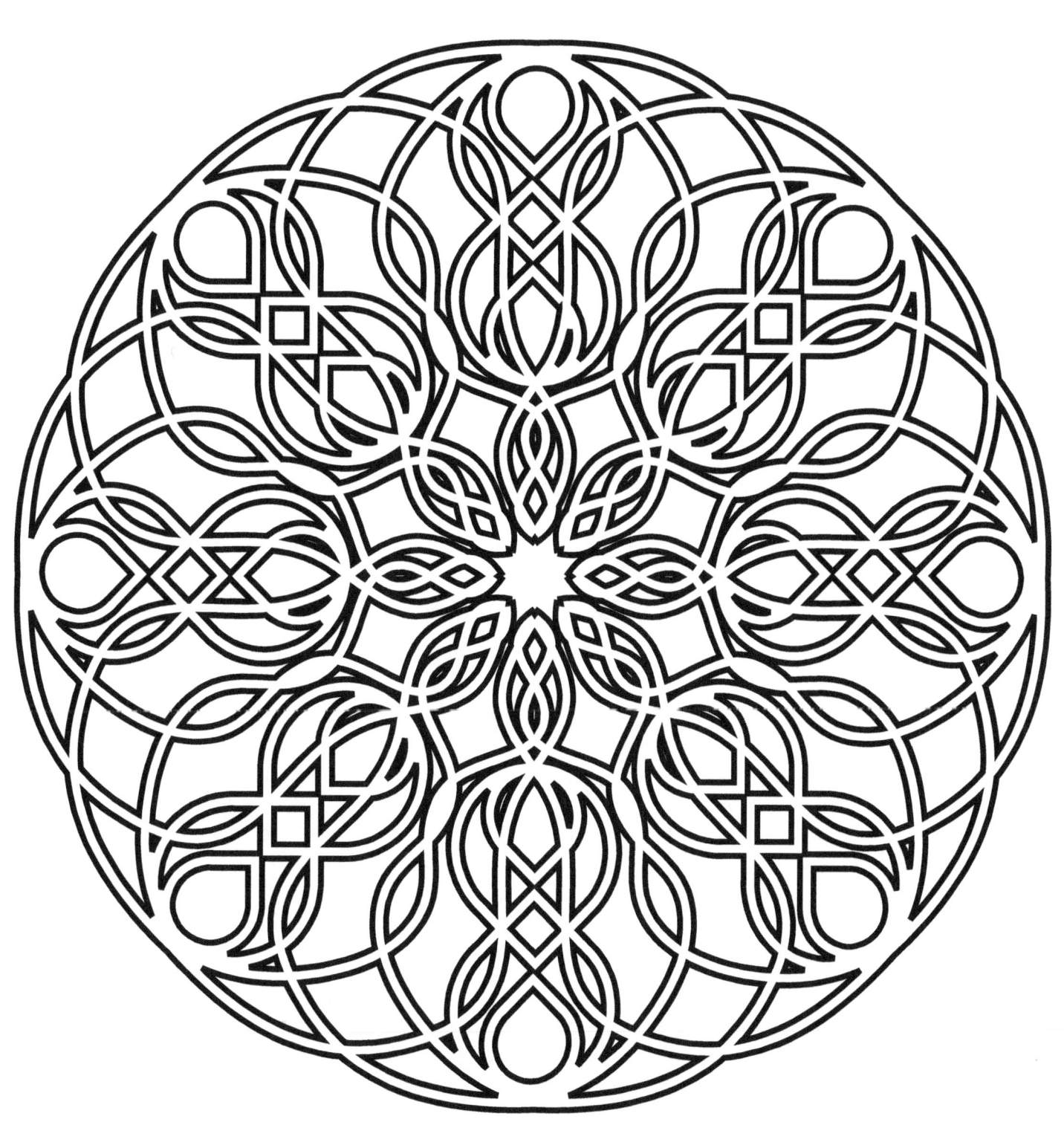

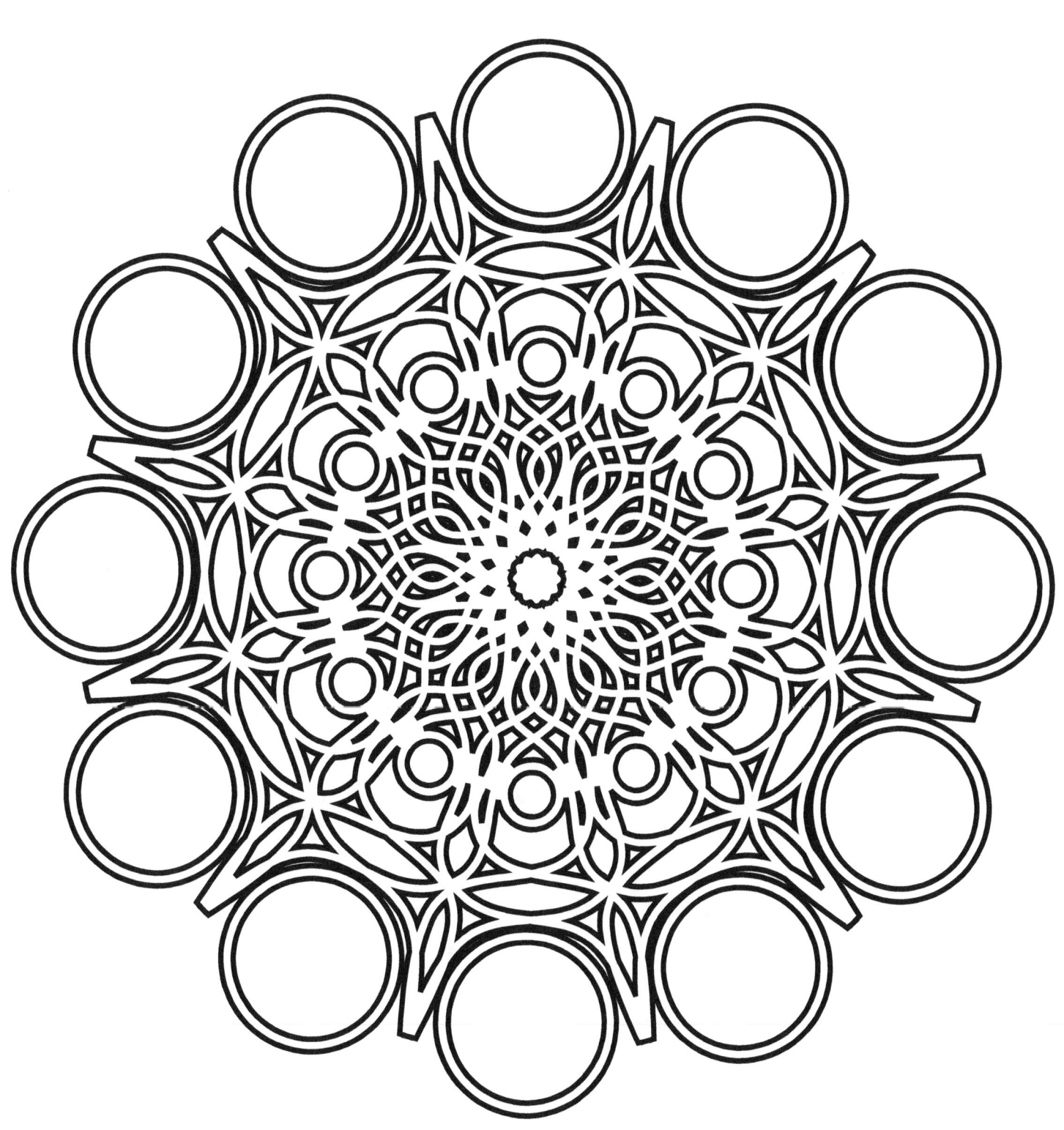

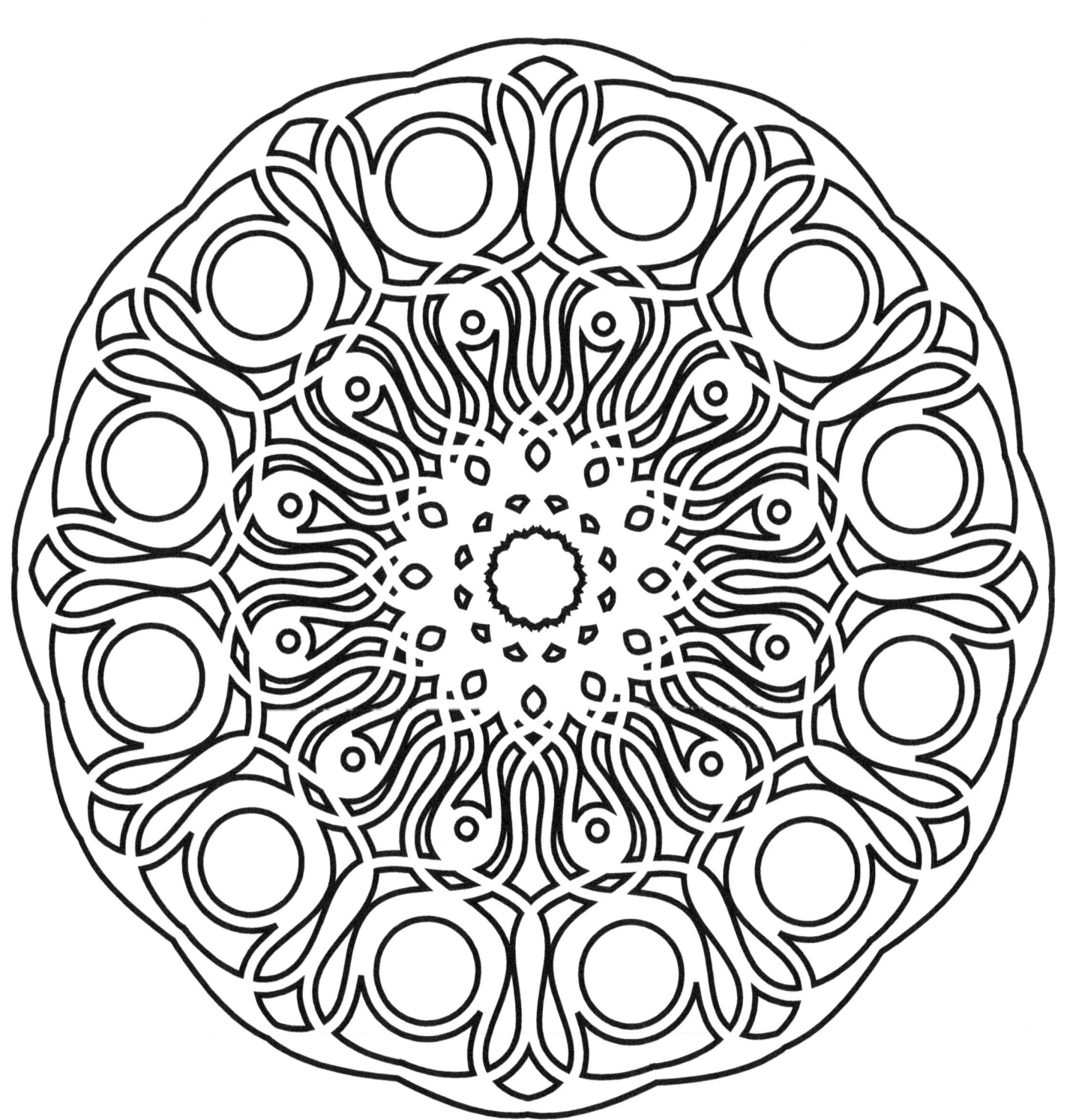

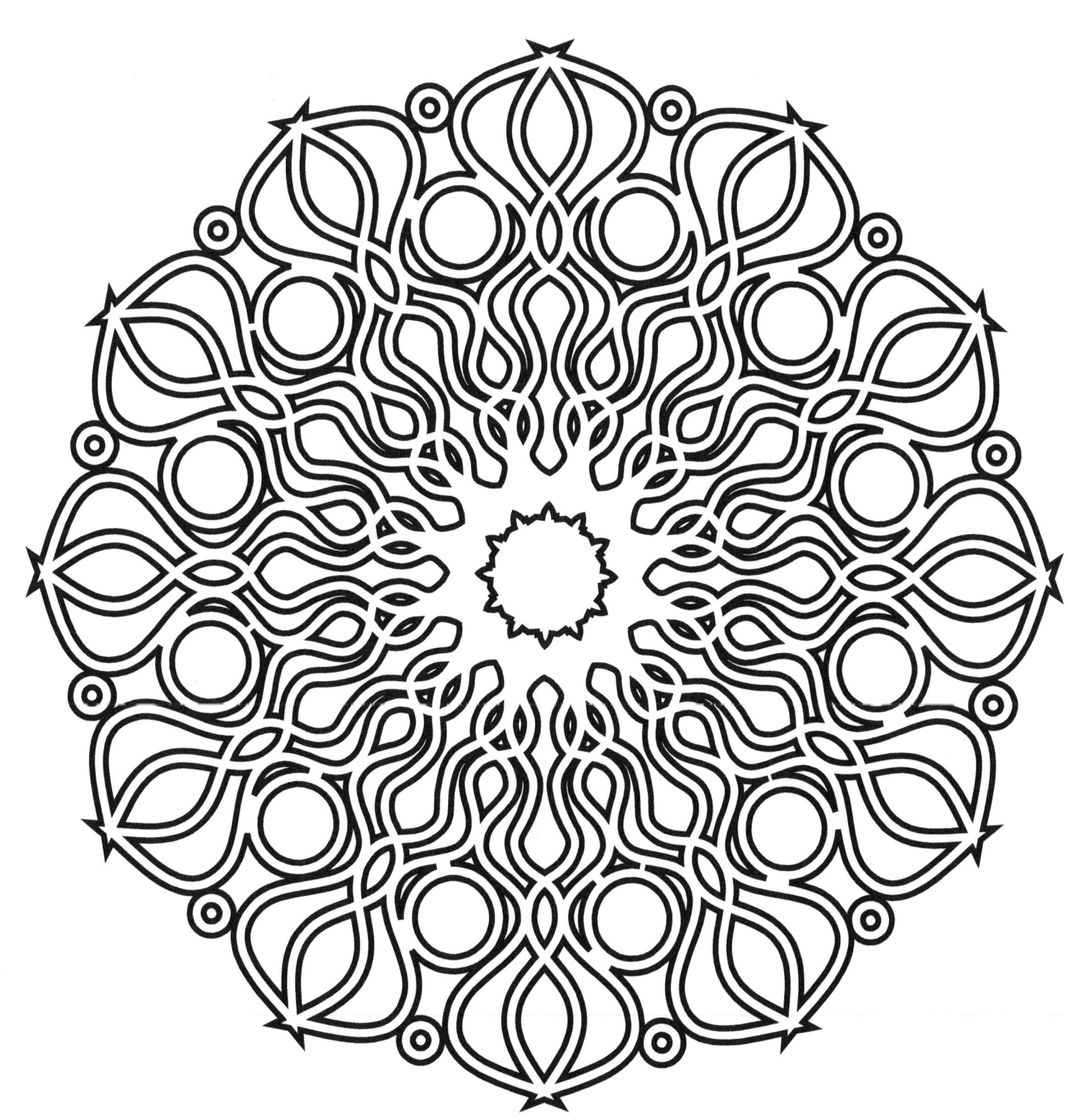

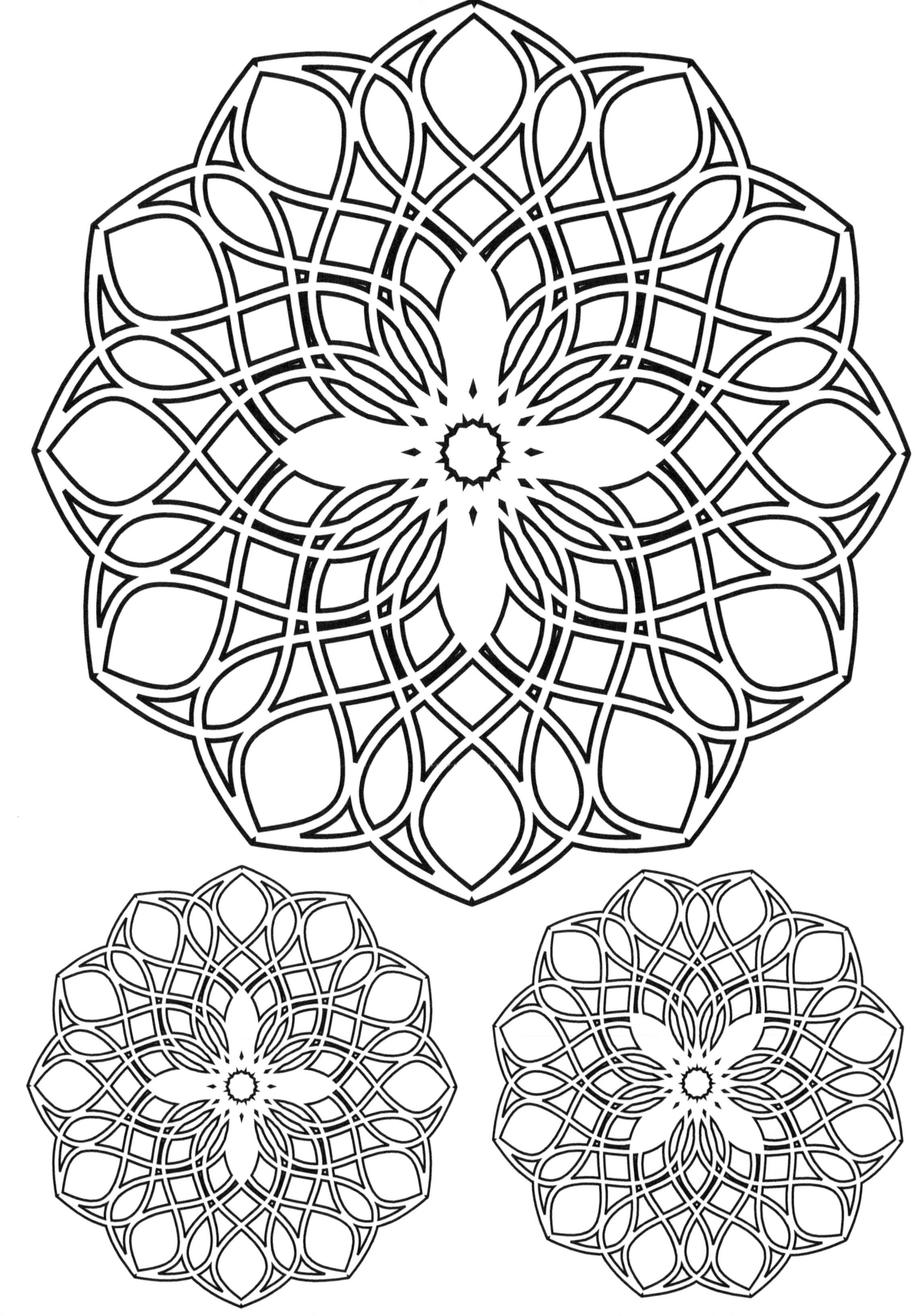

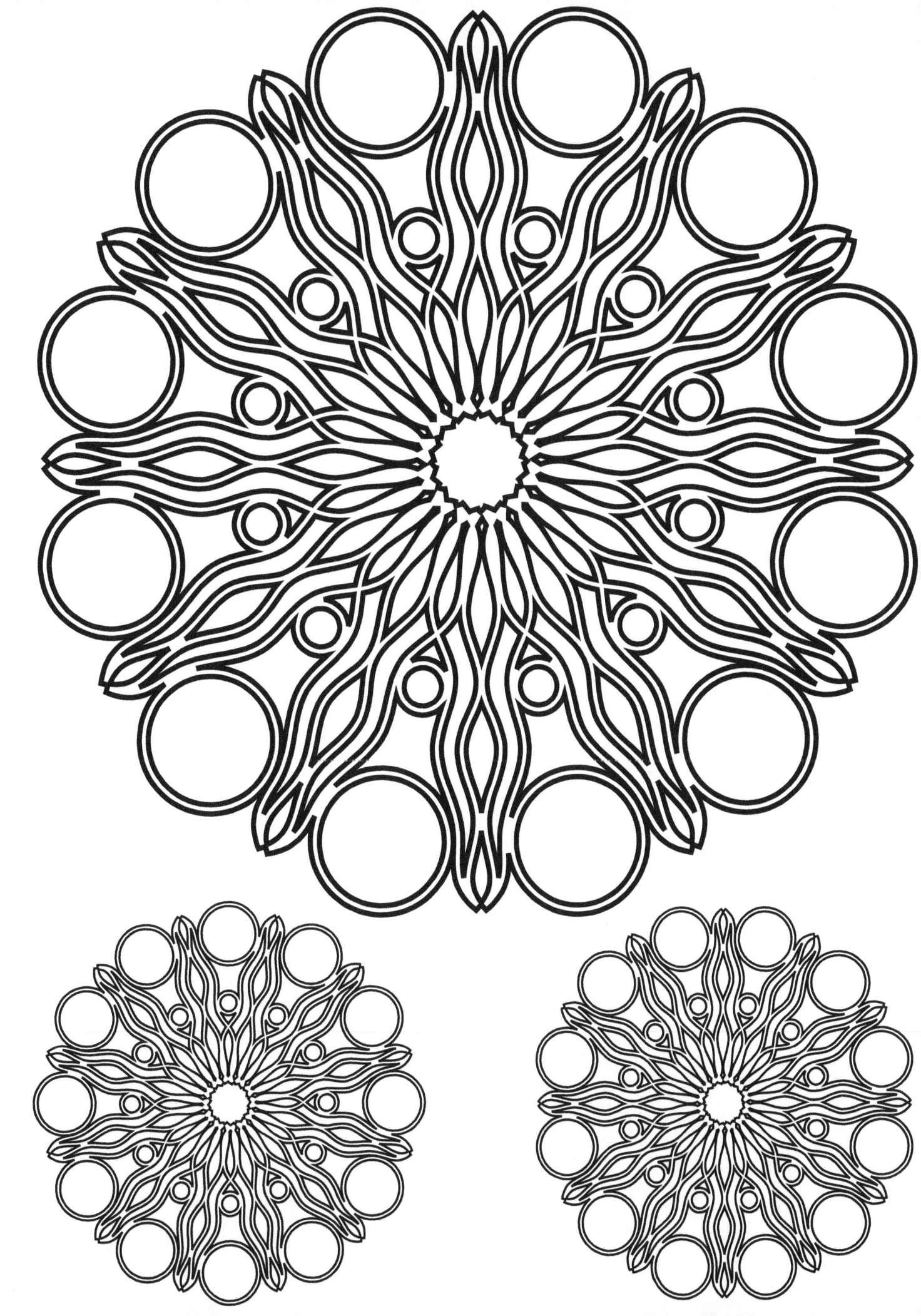

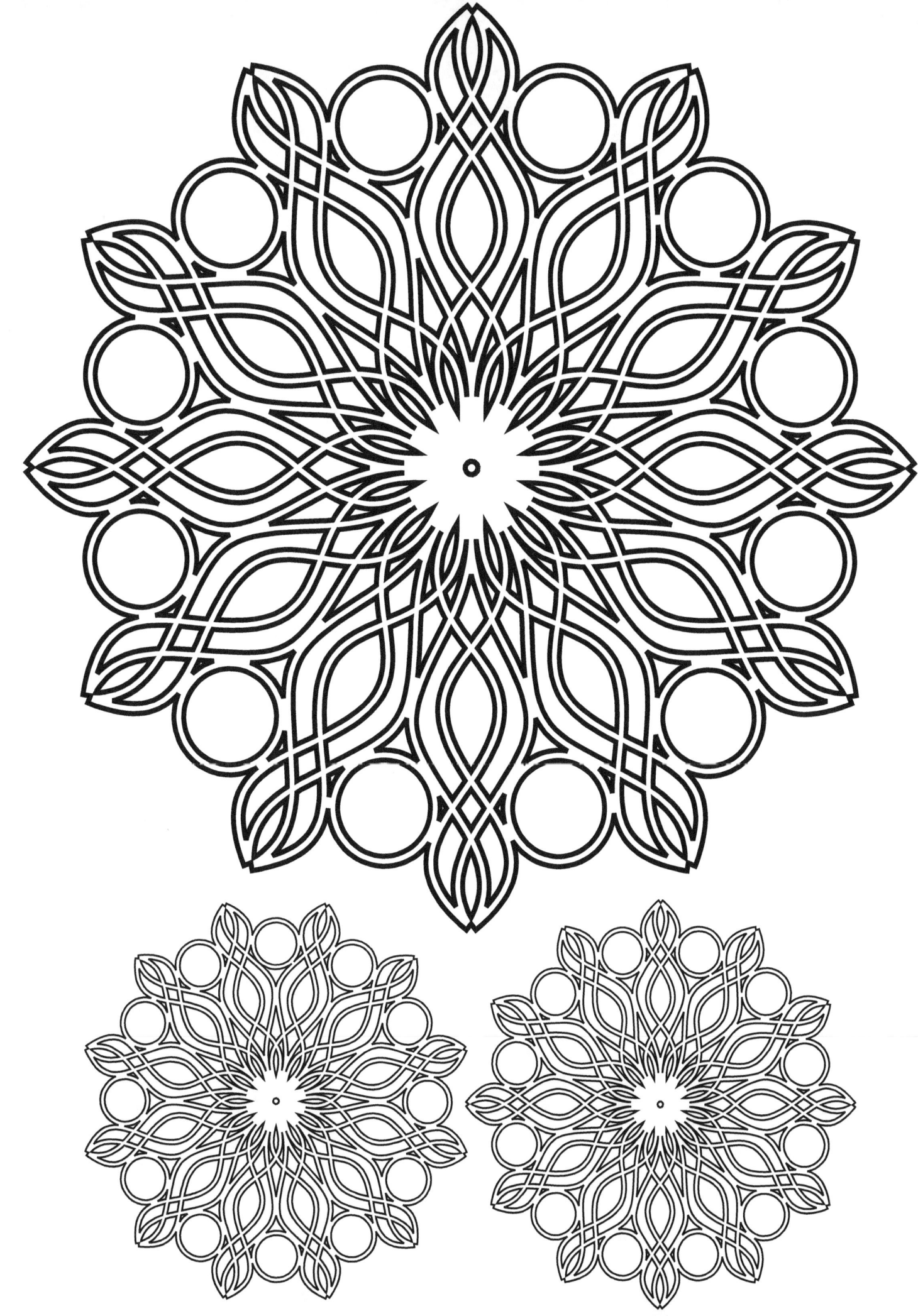

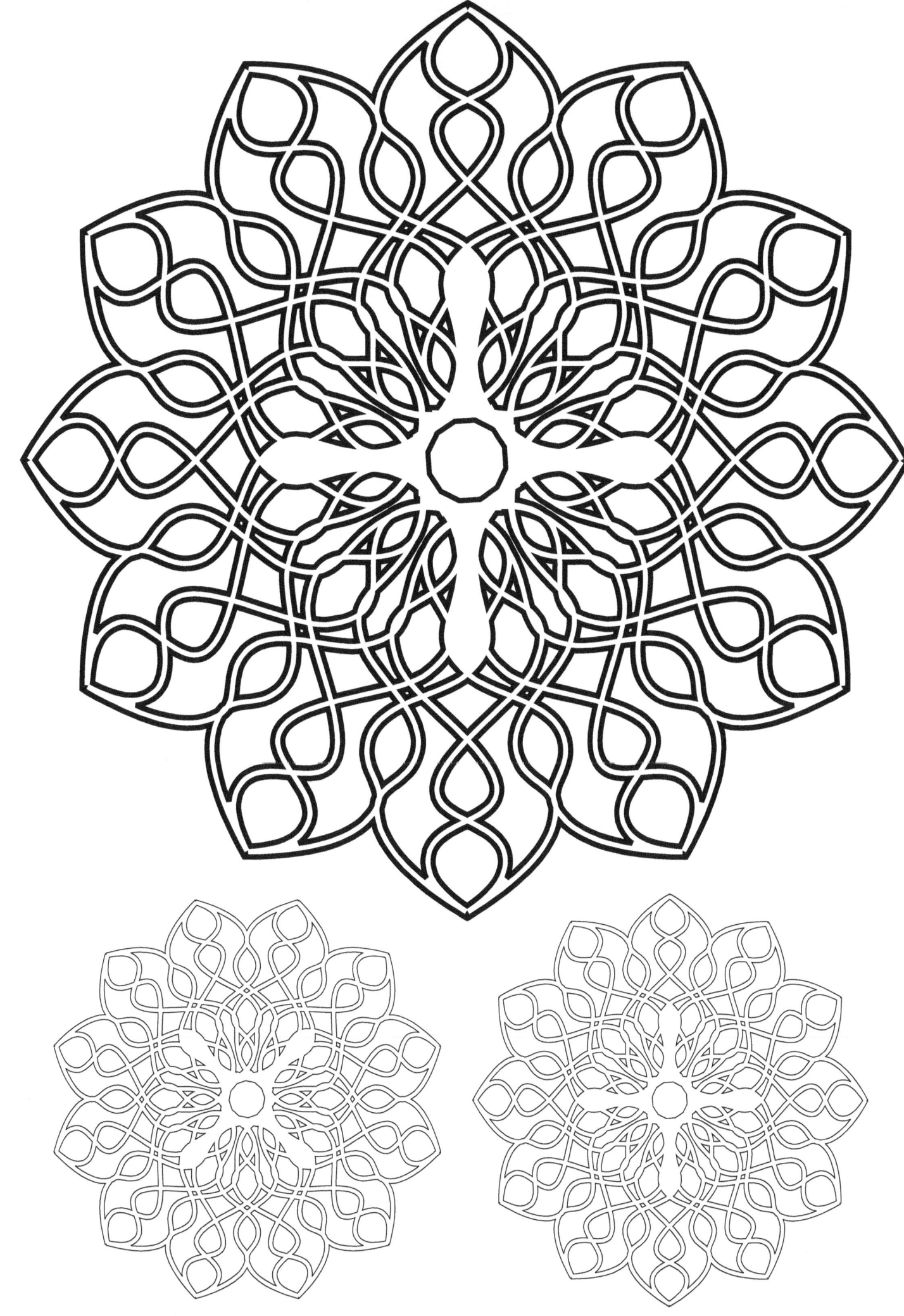

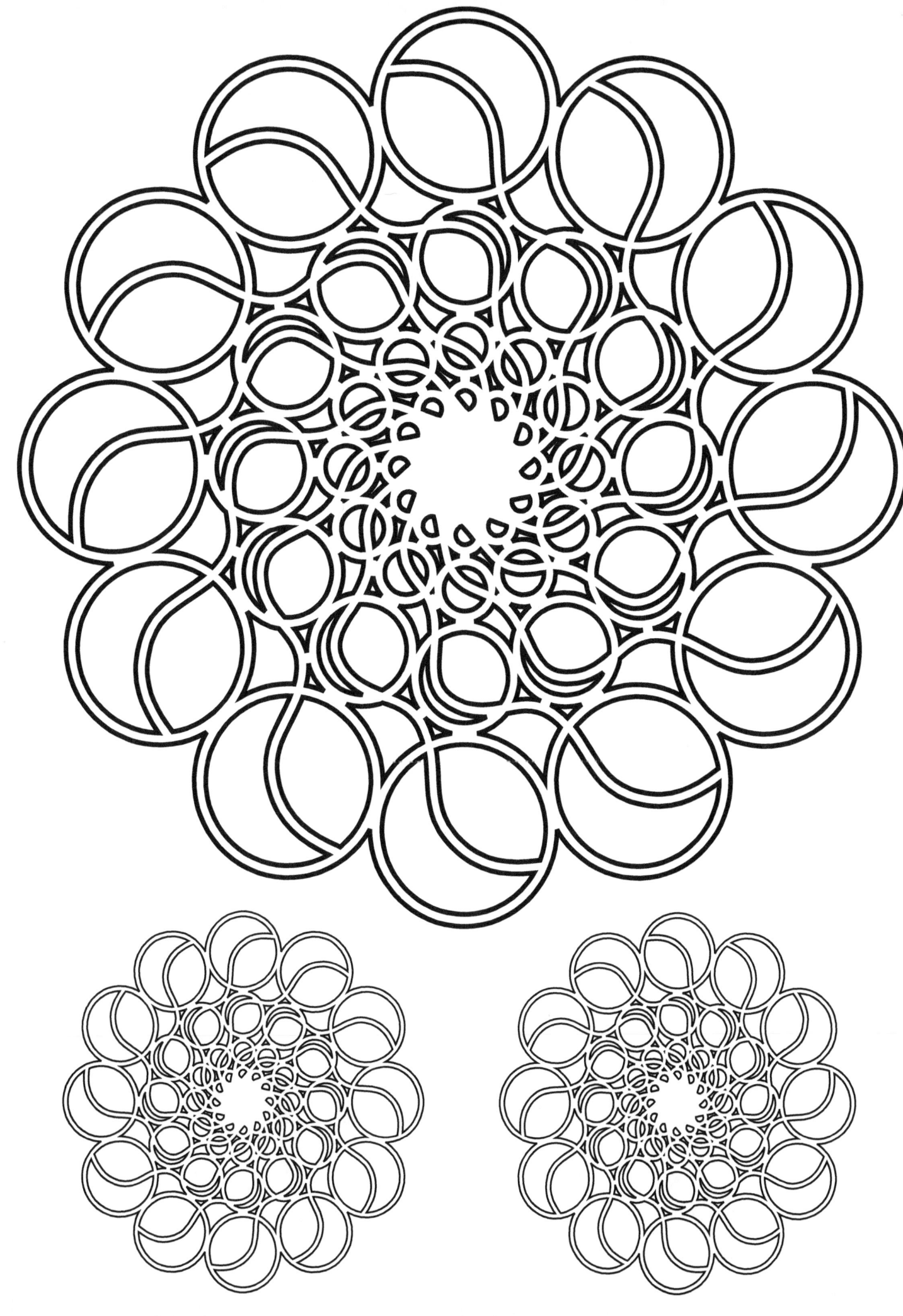

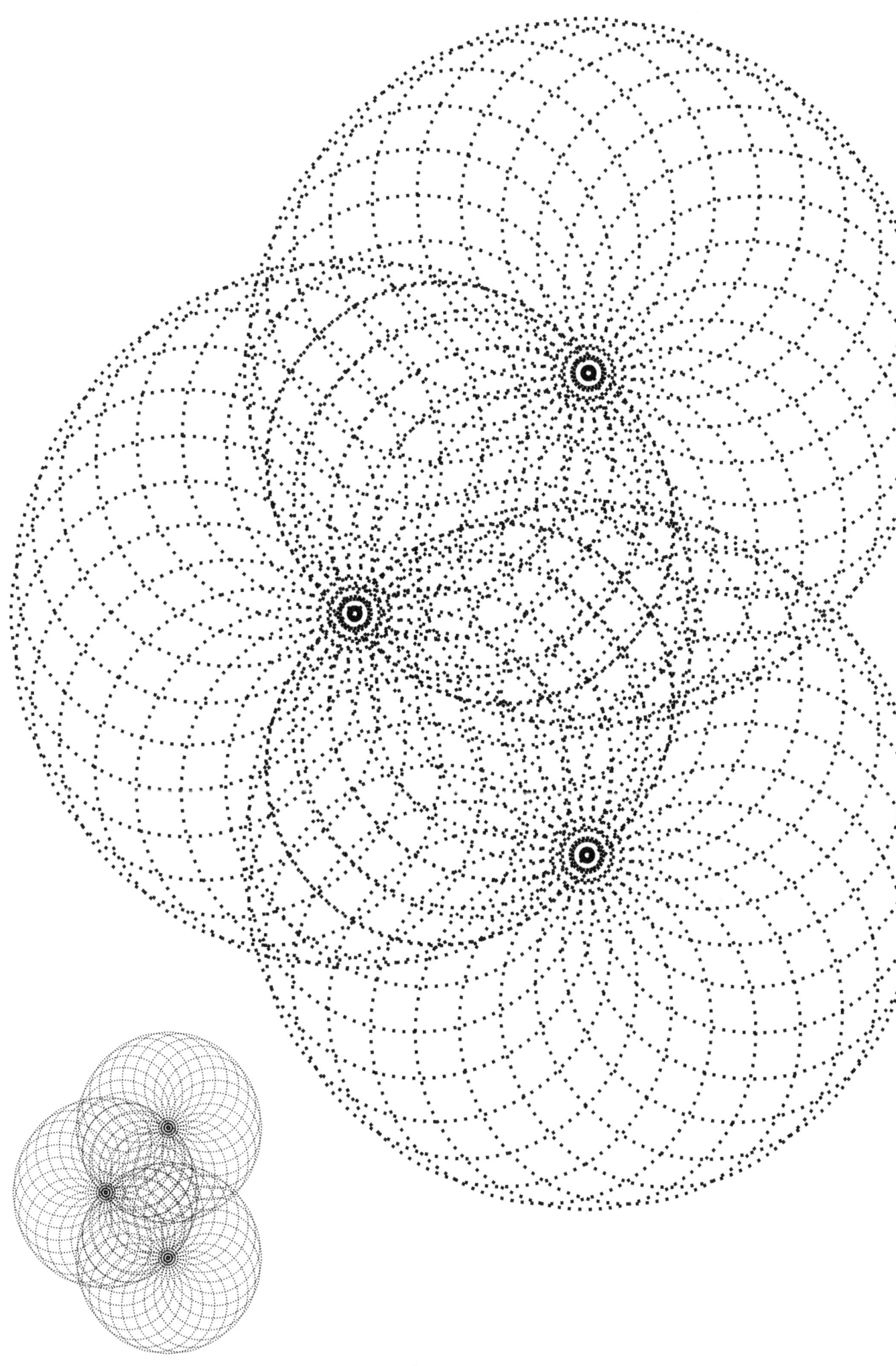

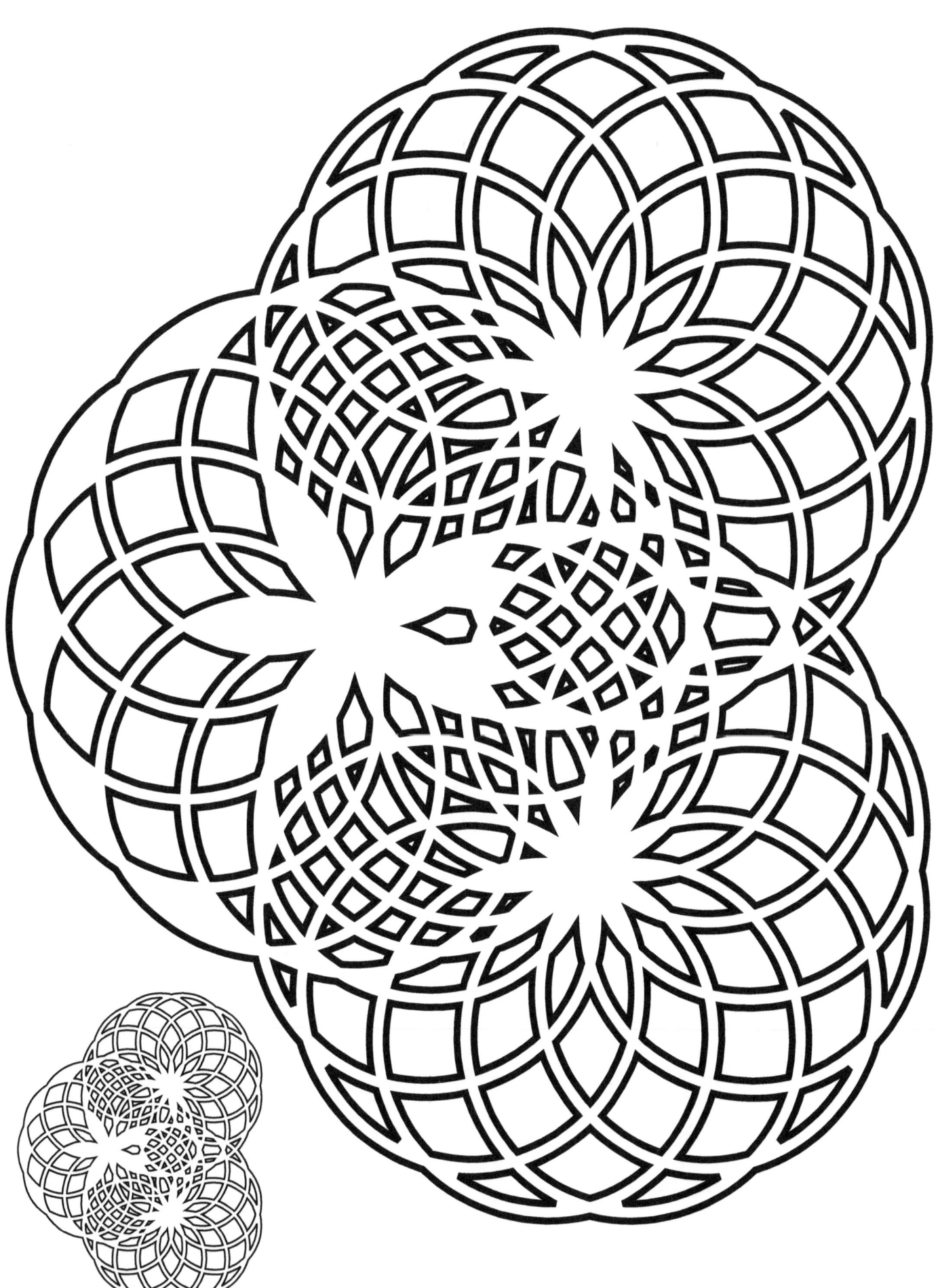

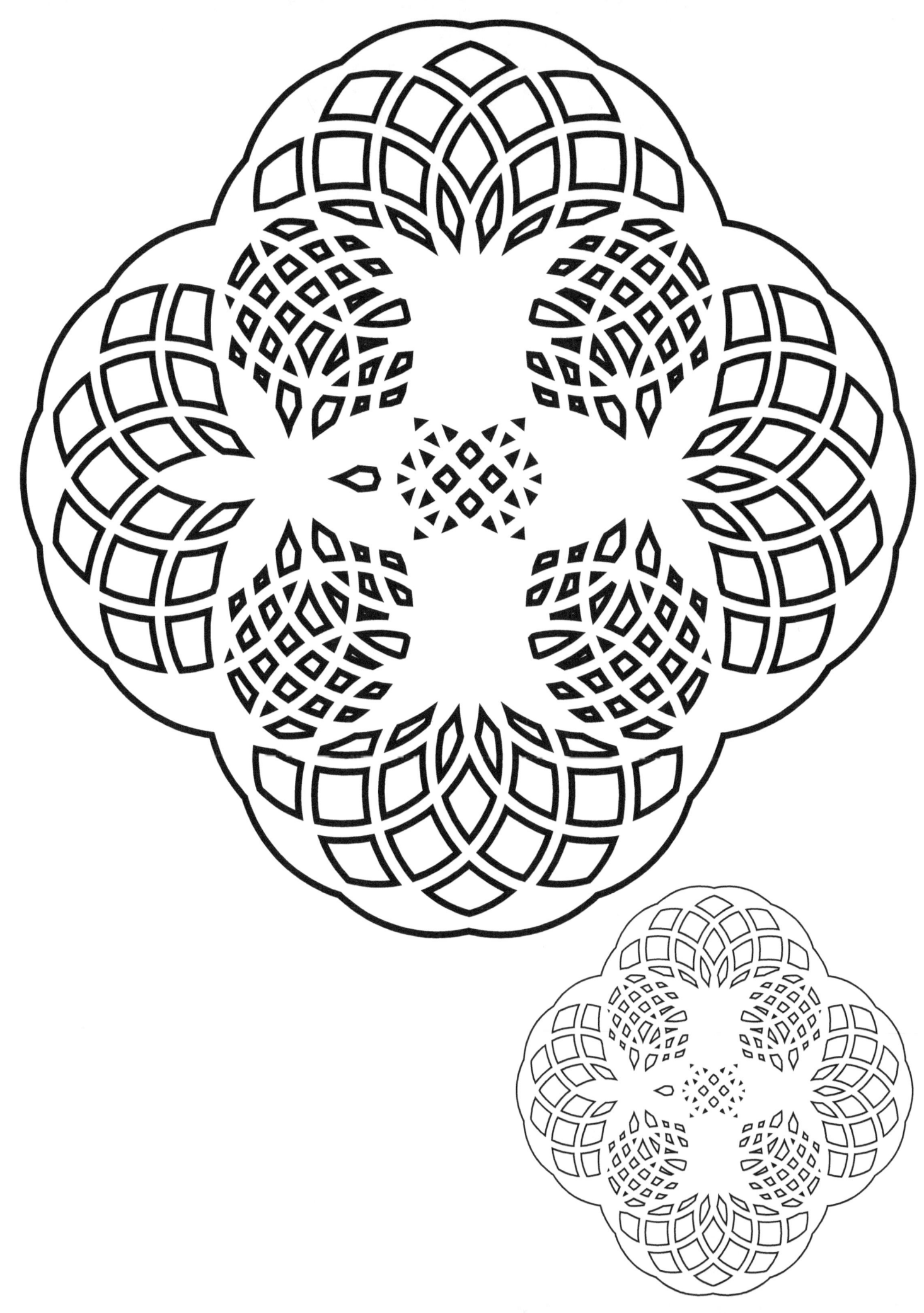

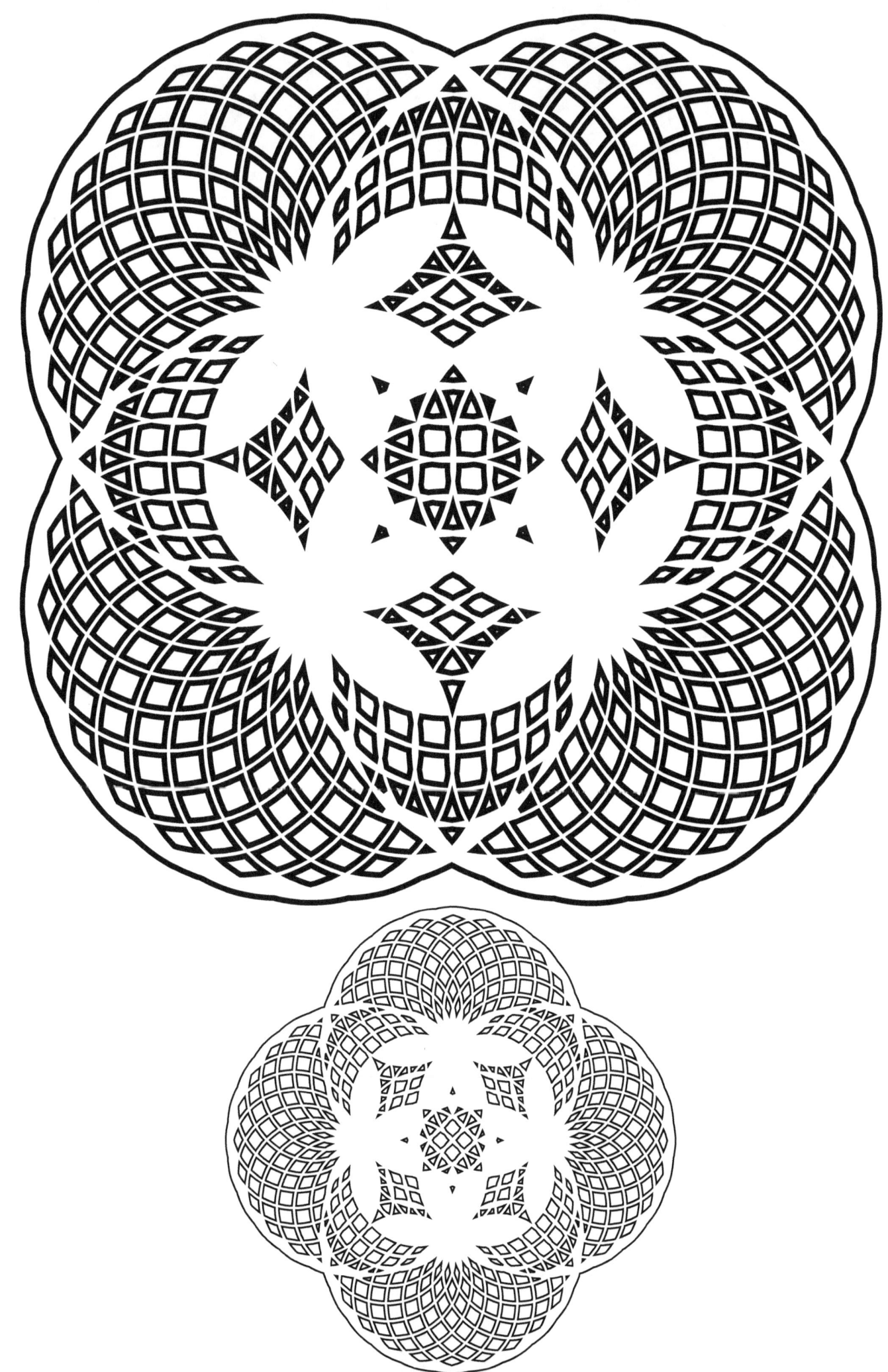

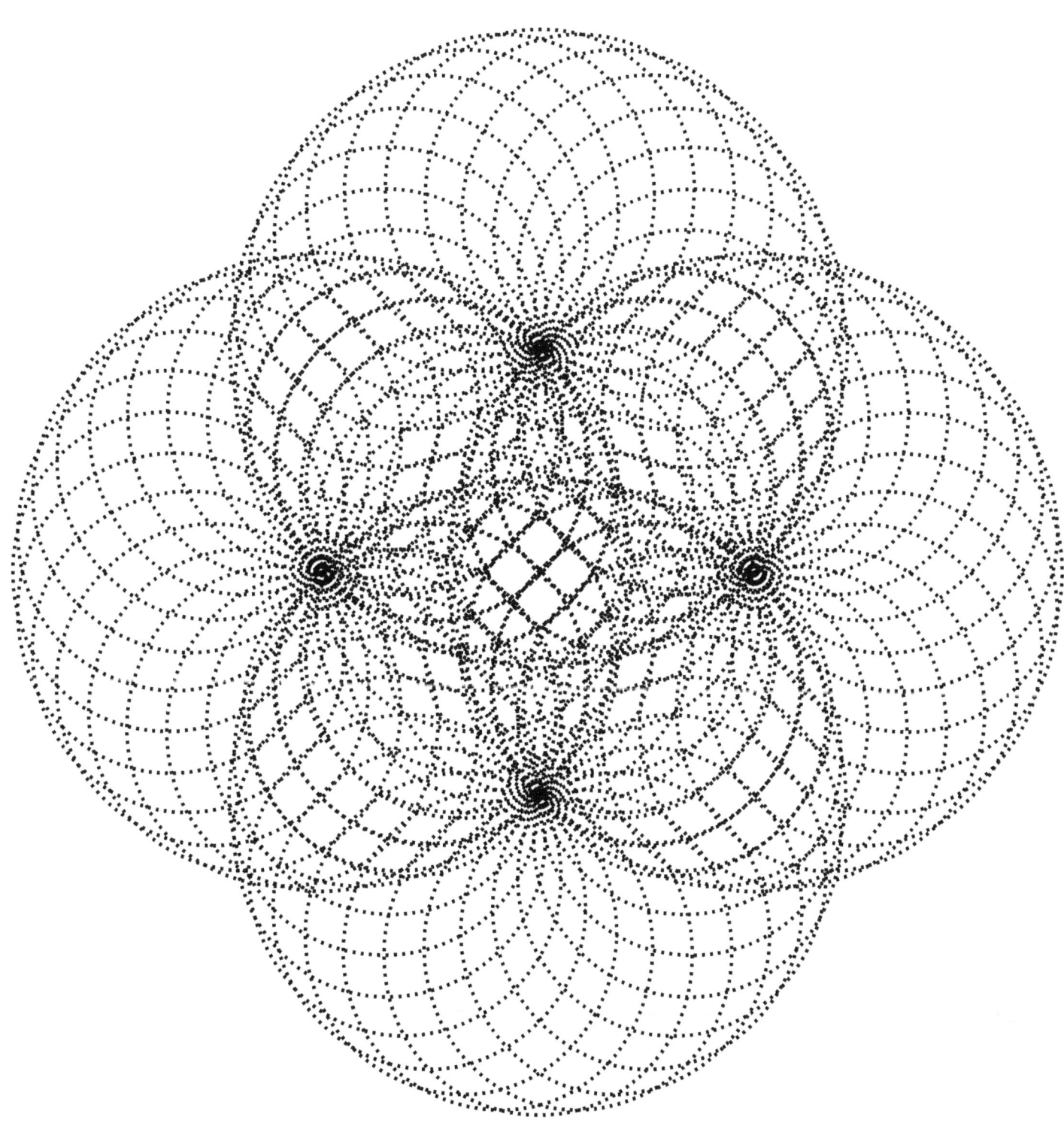

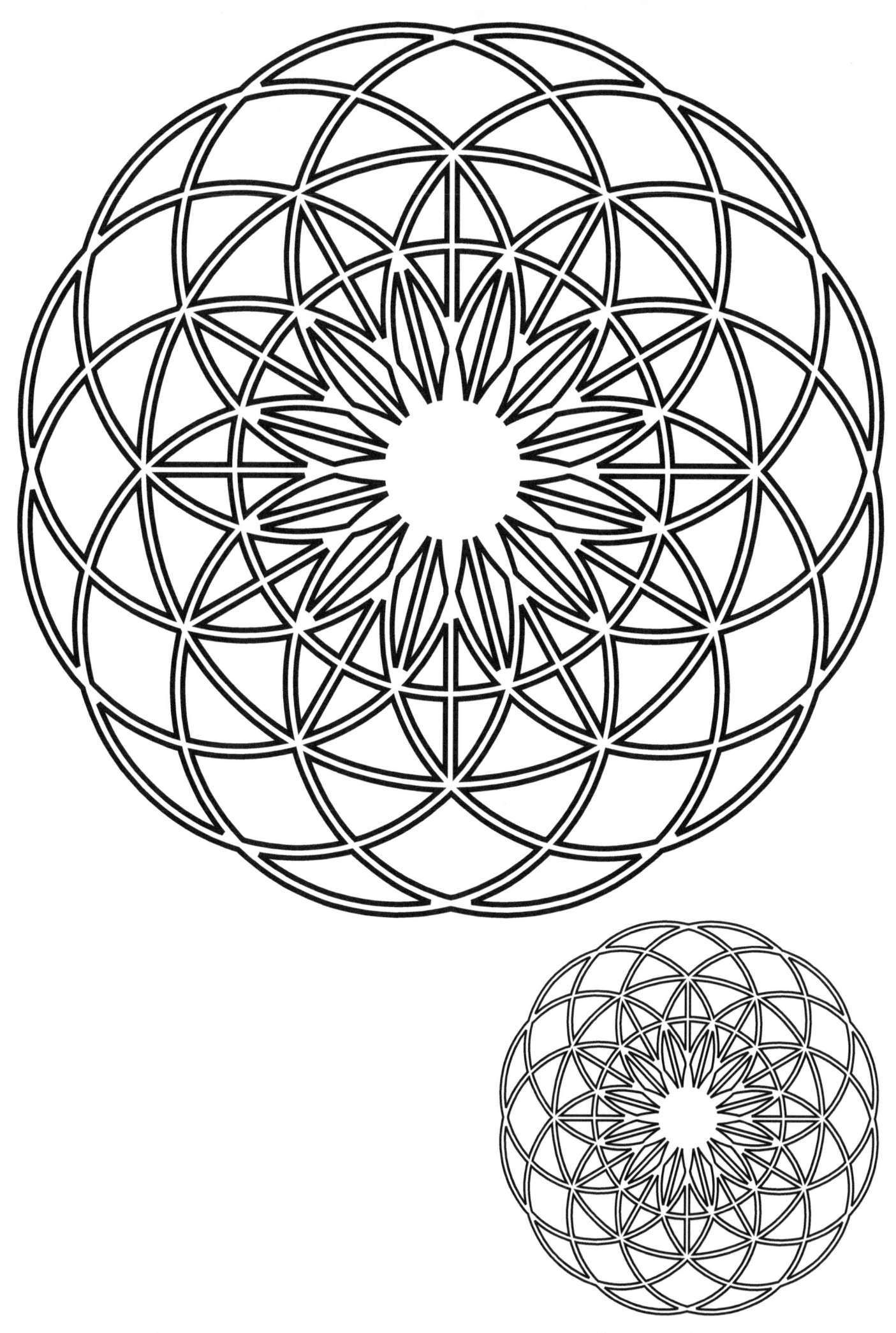

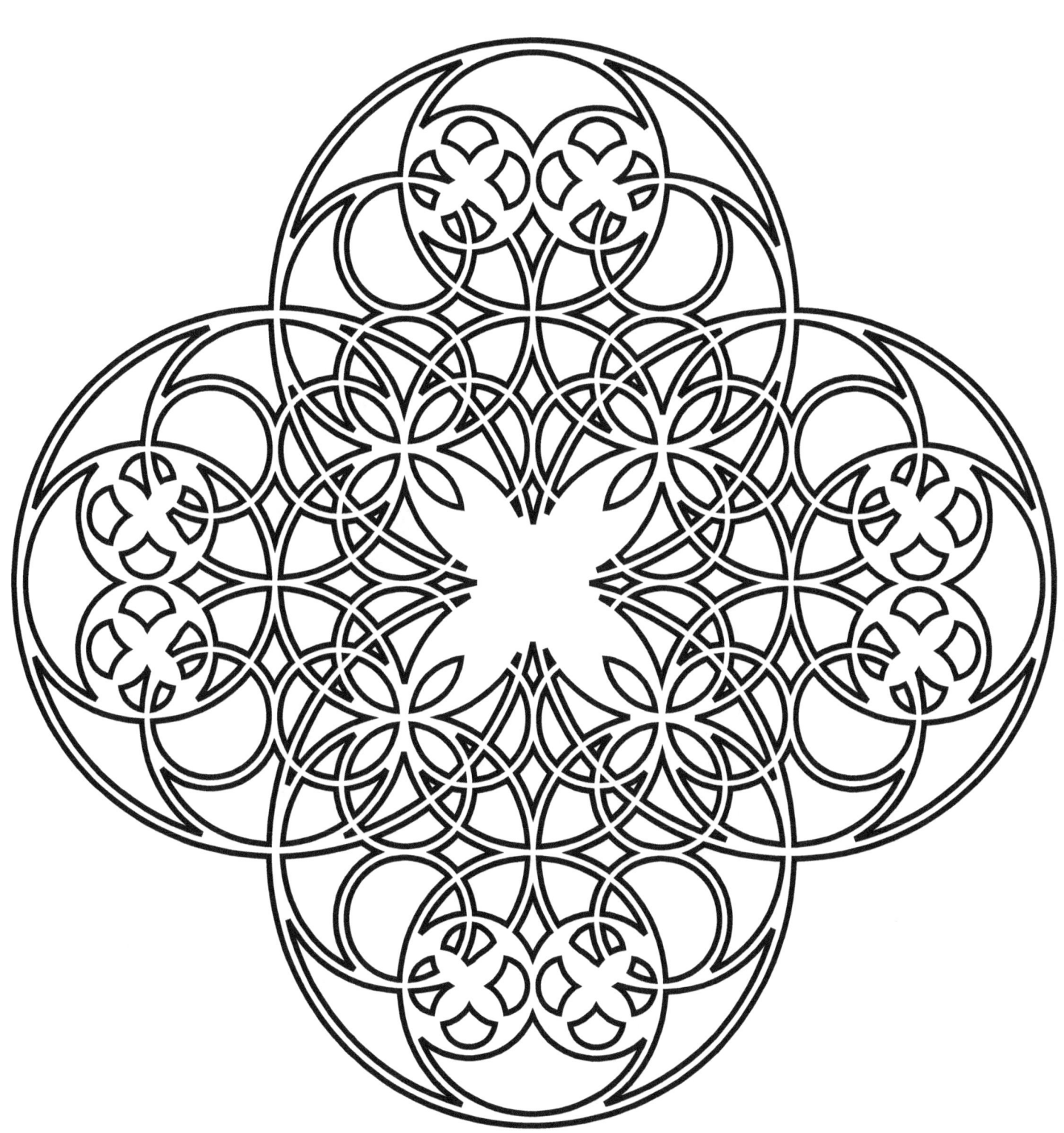

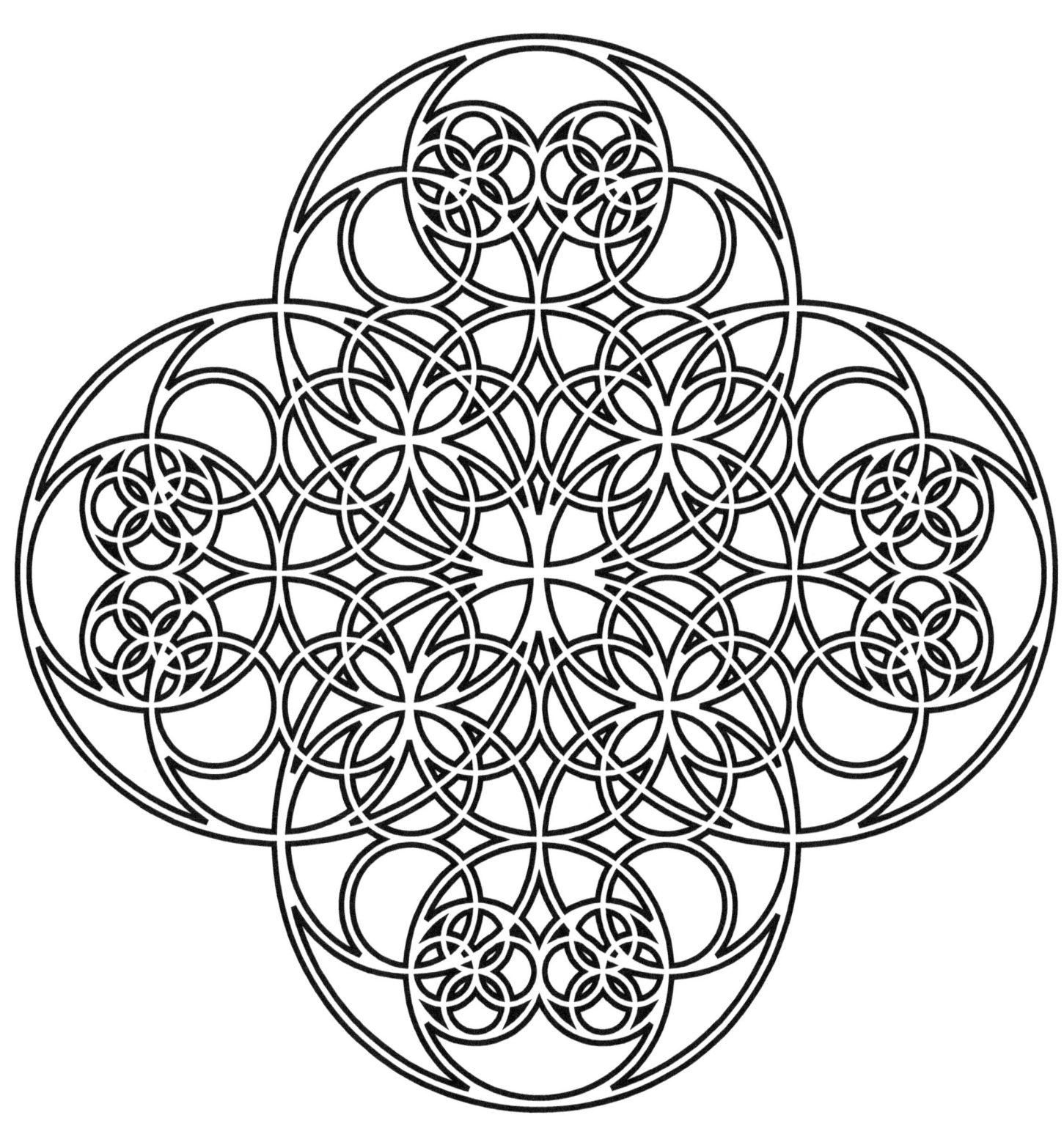

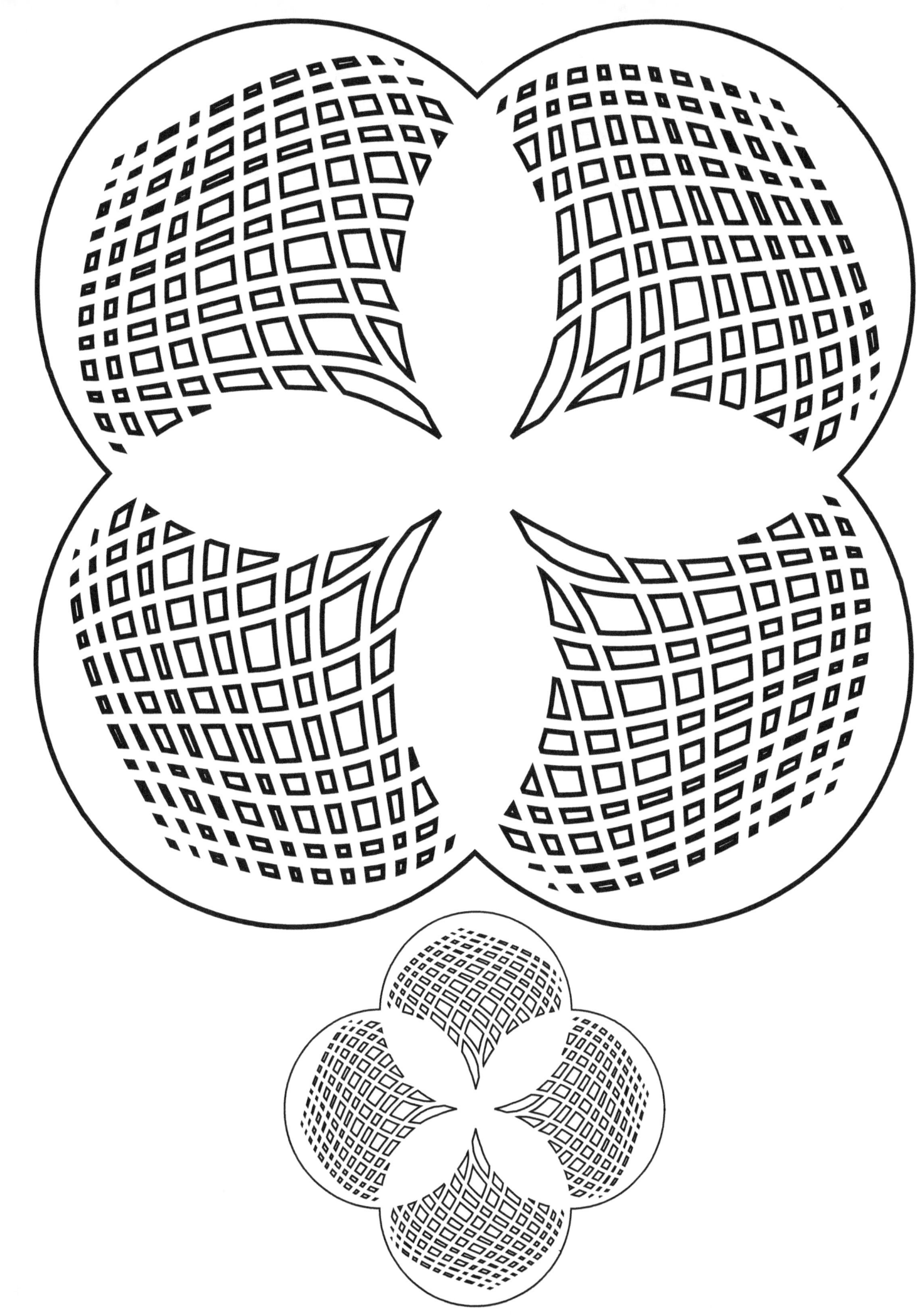

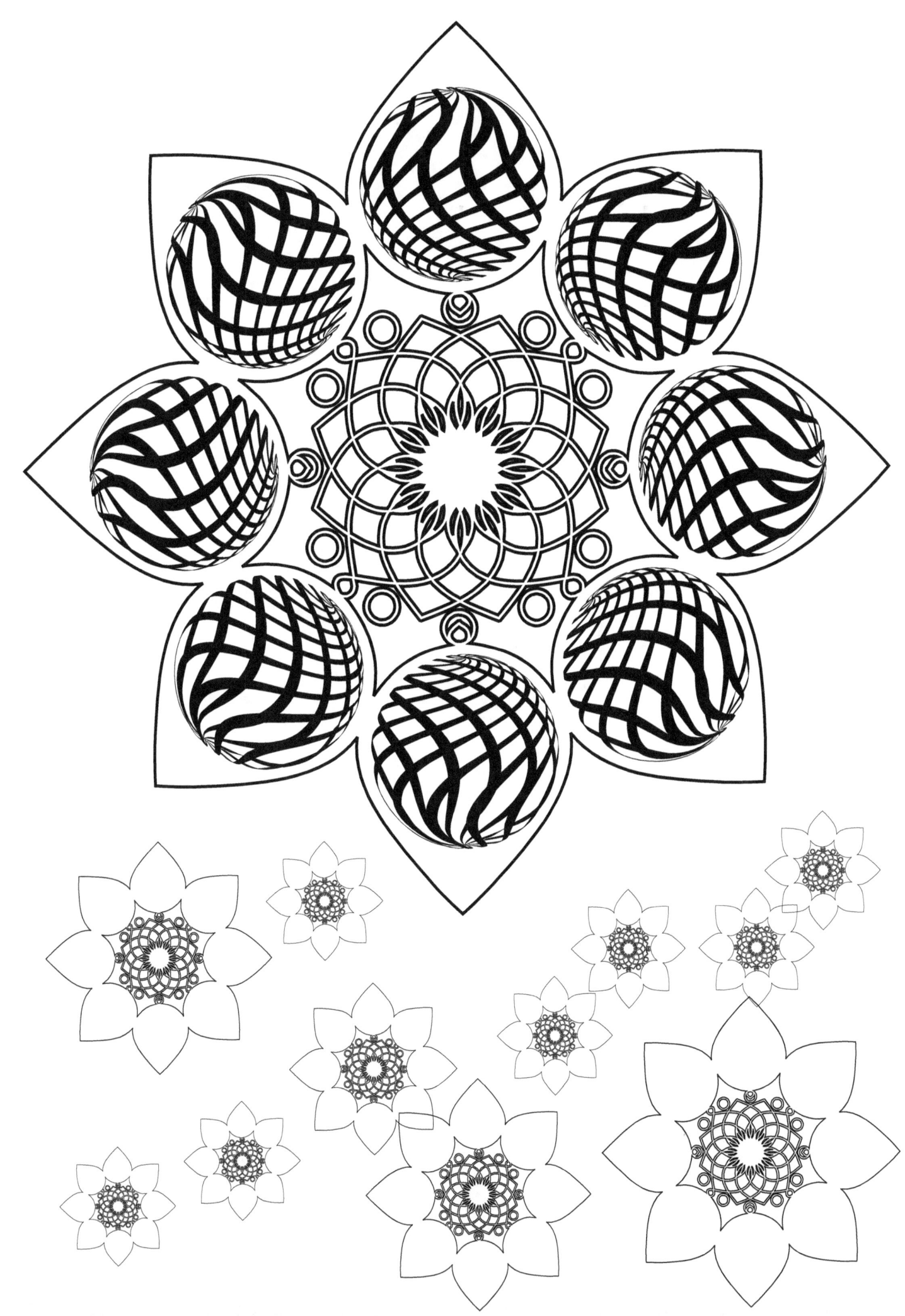

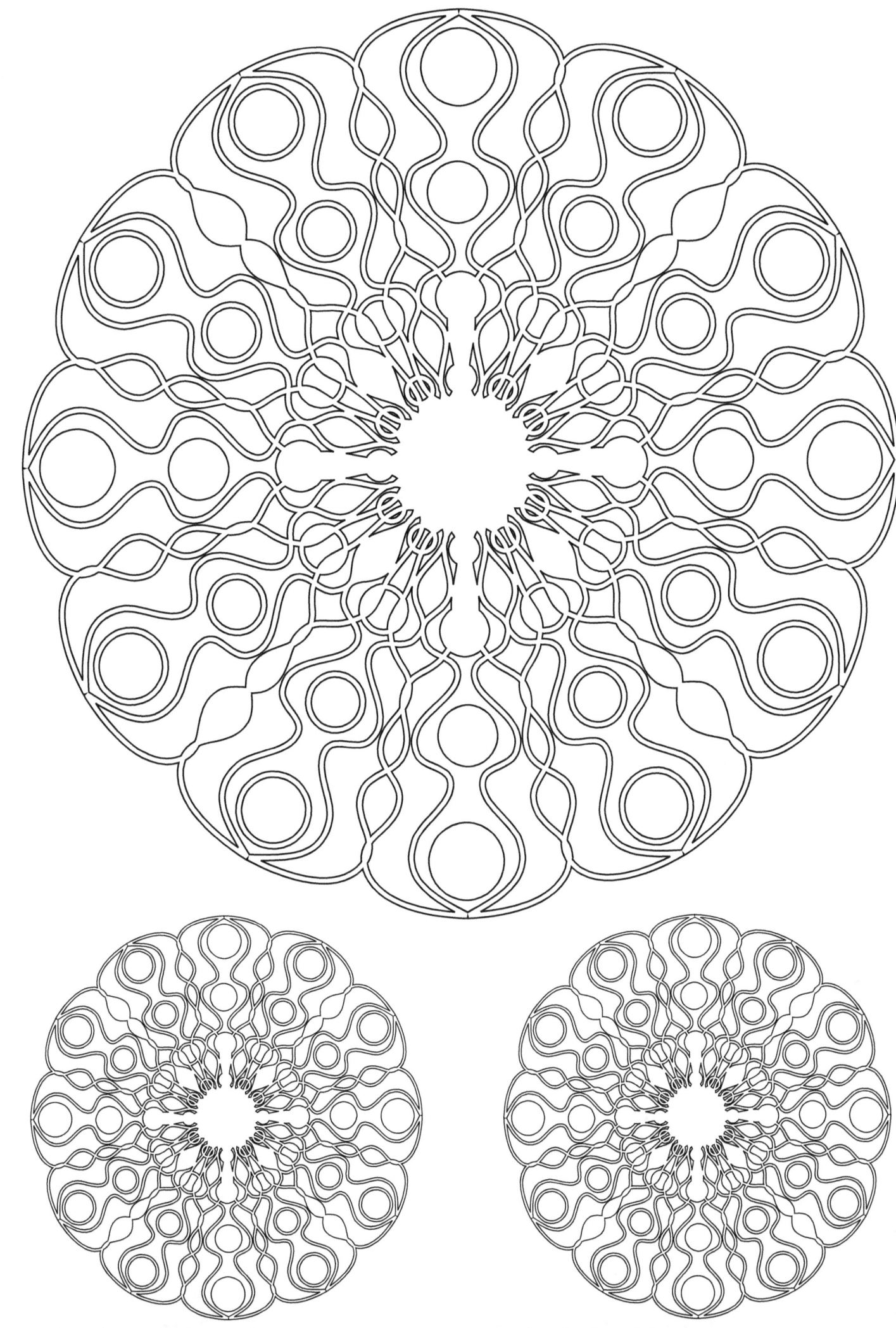

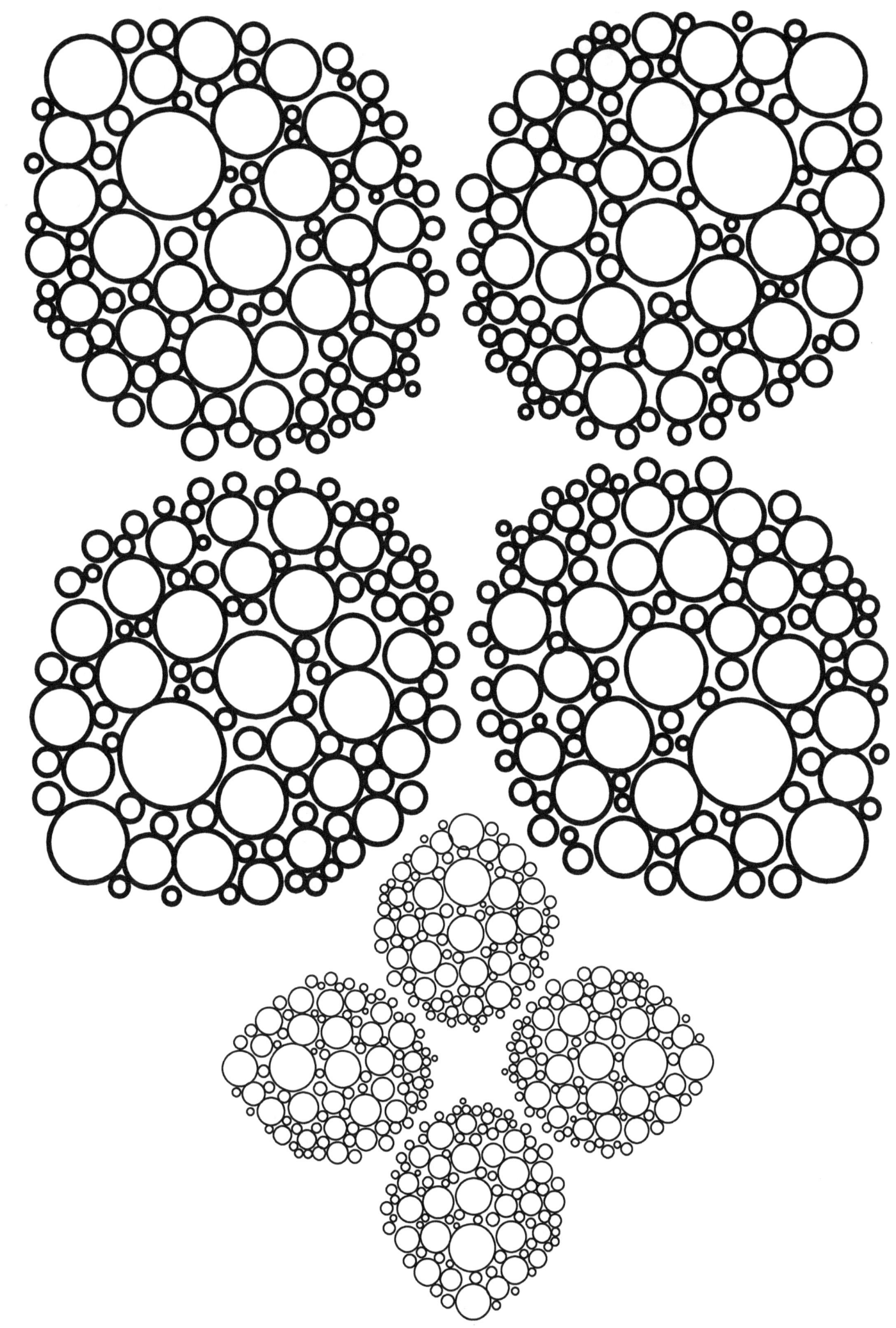

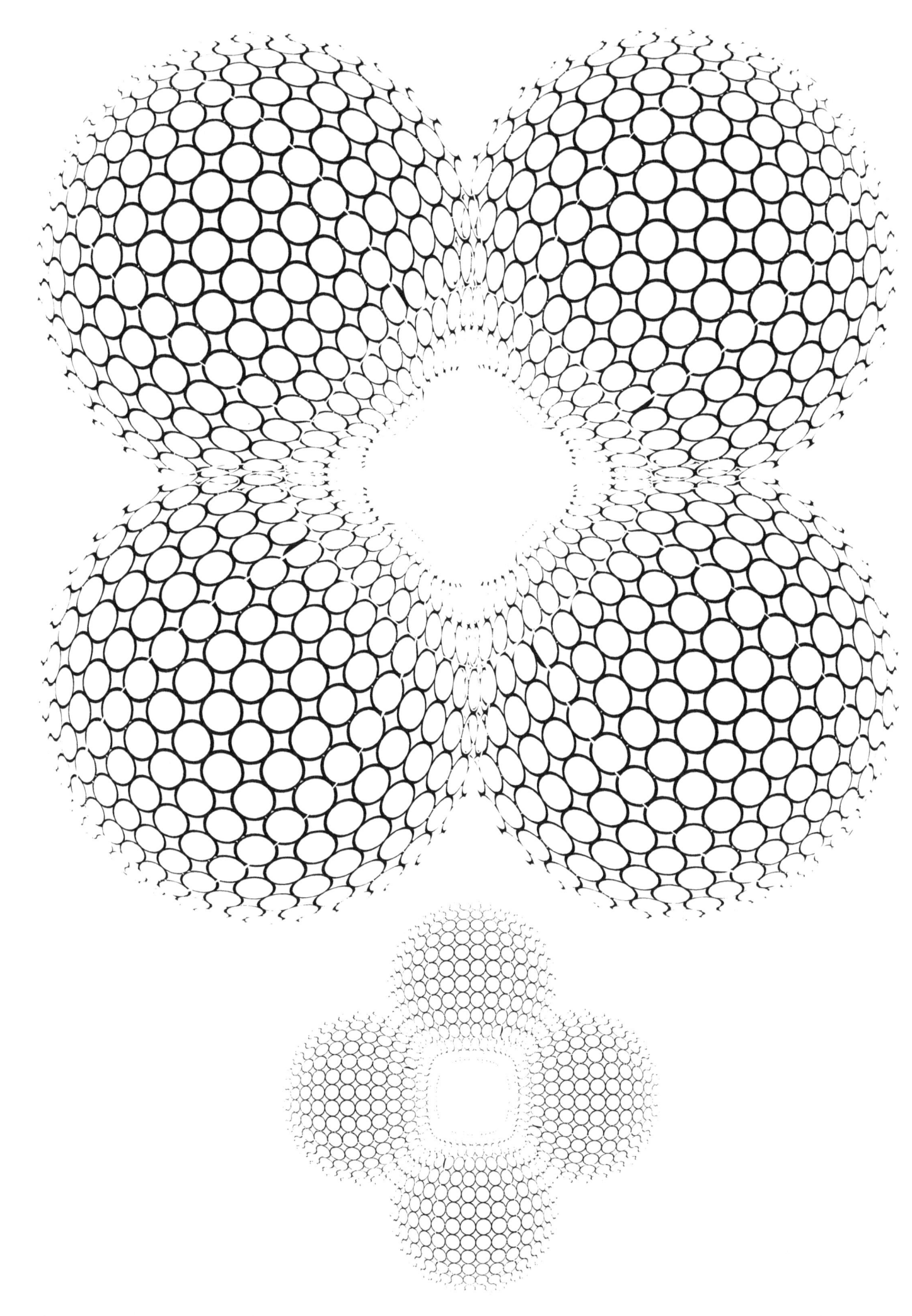

www.ingramcontent.com/pod-product-compliance
Lightning Source LLC
Chambersburg PA
CBHW080710190526
45169CB00006B/2318